Easy Strategies and Lessons That Build Content Area Reading Skills

by Joyce Graham Baltas and Denise Nessel

SCHOLASTIC
PROFESSIONAL BOOKS

NEW YORK • TORONTO • LONDON • AUCKLAND • SYDNEY
MEXICO CITY • NEW DELHI • HONG KONG

**This book is dedicated to
Lauren Rose Graham, a constant source of joy.**

This book grew out of the many conversations we've had with each other about teaching and learning—conversations that focused on strategies we use in our workshops, seminars, and demonstration lessons in schools around the country. We wanted to present some of our favorites along with lesson plans and reading materials that could be used immediately to try the strategies out.

We thank Terry Cooper for her support and guidance in taking the project from the idea stage to a finished product. We also thank the others at Scholastic who provided efficient and effective help in the design and production of the book: Virginia Dooley and Ellen Ungaro.

We'd also like to acknowledge the school districts in which we've been working most recently. Teachers have welcomed us into their classrooms, watched us teach, let us watch them, tried our suggestions, and gave us valuable feedback about what works and what doesn't. They've kept us grounded in the realities of the classroom while sharing our vision of more engaging instruction based on more effective teaching strategies. This book reflects their influences. Their students, in their responses to our teaching, have also taught us a great deal. In particular, we'd like to recognize the teachers and students of these districts: Beacon, New York; Dayton, Ohio; Freeport, Illinois; Indianapolis, Indiana; Milwaukee, Wisconsin; and Prince George's County, Maryland.

Finally, we'd like to acknowledge our colleagues and fellow consultants in the National Urban Alliance for Effective Education. Our ongoing work within NUA has given us invaluable opportunities to learn from and share with a terrific group of master teachers who are dedicated to providing the very best in professional development for teachers and administrators. We hope this book will serve to bring more people into the NUA circle to share the vision of improving the educational experience for all students and for students in urban schools in particular.

Cover design by Jaime Lucero

Interior design by Sarah Morrow

Interior photos and illustrations: Women's Suffrage Statue (page 13): AP Photo/Tyler Mallory. Susan B. Anthony (page 14): Library of Congress. New Dehli (page 29): AP Photo/John Moore. Craig Kielburger (page 31): AP Photo/Tom Hanson. Mountain Climbers (page 39): Photo Disc. Mountain Climbers (page 40): Photo Disc. Train (page 47): Digital Stock. Jackie Robinson (page 55): Cornelius Van Wright. Theodore Roosevelt, Abraham Lincoln (page 63), Franklin Roosevelt, John Kennedy (page 64), and Bill Clinton (page 65): Library of Congress. Grey Wolf (page 73): Photo Disc. Ellis Island (page 84): Library of Congress. Visa (page 84): Photo Disc. Leonardo DaVinci (Page 93) AP Photo/Biblioteca Reale, Turin.

ISBN 0-439-04092-2

Contents

Introduction

When students move from the primary grades to the upper elementary grades and beyond, they are expected to read a greater variety of informational material such as science or social studies text books, encyclopedias or other reference materials, and a variety of other information resources, including newspapers, magazines, and websites. This focus on reading to learn, often called content area reading, poses new challenges for students and teachers.

Science and social studies textbooks may be so dense with concepts that students have a hard time comprehending the material, especially if they've had little first-hand experience with the topic. Even if students have relevant prior knowledge, a material's overall reading level or style of writing may be too difficult for many students to handle. Also, if the topics themselves do not seem particularly interesting, students will not be drawn into the reading, curious to know more.

For these reasons, it's usually a struggle to make content-area reading interesting and engaging. Some teachers have students take turns reading the text aloud and then pose questions to check their understanding. Others read the text to the students, explaining and discussing page by page. While these practices ensure that all students read or hear the same material and answer the same questions, they do not necessarily result in good comprehension and concept development.

In our work as consultants in schools across the United States, we're often asked for effective ways to approach content area reading. In this book, we present ten strategies that we use successfully for this purpose. These strategies involve the use of activities before, during, and after reading that make informational texts more accessible to students. Though each strategy is different, all aim to keep students interested in the topic and actively involved in learning new information.

These ten strategies help students read more purposefully, think more carefully about vocabulary and concepts, and make connections between what they already know and what they are learning. When teachers use these strategies consistently, over time, students' comprehension and thinking abilities will increase, and they'll enjoy reading much more, too.

In each chapter, you'll find an introduction to a strategy, guidelines for using the strategy in your classroom, and activities to do before, during, or after reading. You'll also find a complete model lesson that includes a reproducible reading selection, reproducible student page, and follow-up activities. The strategies featured include: Anticipation Guides, Key Words, Key Words II, Facts and Inferences, List•Group•Label, News Flash, Possible Sentences, Read•Talk•Write, Strip Story, and Team Webbing.

To get started, read through the book to become familiar with the different strategies. Then select one strategy you wish to try with your students. After you have taught the lesson, evaluate it. Think about: "What worked? What could I change the next time I try this strategy? What did my students do well? What could they do better? How can I help them do this better? How can I use this strategy in other content areas? What materials will I need to ensure success?" Then plan other lessons using the same strategy and materials from your classroom. You should keep using this strategy with a variety of texts until you are comfortable with it and your students know it.

Then select another new strategy to learn and use with your students. Try this one until it becomes part of your teaching repertoire and then add another new one. Continue this process until you have incorporated all ten strategies into your teaching. As you try them in your classroom, keep the following suggestions in mind:

5

- Do not get discouraged if a strategy doesn't work the first time. Reflect on what worked and didn't work during the lesson and then try it again.

- Share the strategies with other teachers. Plan lessons together and discuss your results after teaching the lesson.

- Don't stop after you have tried one or two strategies. Keep going until you have learned all ten.

- Use the strategies consistently and often over the school year.

- Try the strategies with many different types of text including books, magazines, articles, videos, and more.

We hope you find these strategies as effective and useful as we have.

Anticipation Guides

Strategy Summary

An anticipation guide is a set of statements concerning the topic students will be reading about. Students read and either agree or disagree with each statement before reading the assigned article. Some of the statements are true and some are false, but the correct answers aren't obvious. After discussing and debating their ideas, students read to get more information. Then they review their initial responses, revising them as needed. This strategy sparks lively discussion, sharpens students' reasoning skills, and provides clear and compelling purposes for reading informational text.

Before Reading

- Tell students what the topic is and hand out the anticipation guide. Have them work in small groups to respond to each item. Remind them to be prepared to explain their reasoning.

- Make students feel comfortable about not having the right answers or even much information about the topic. Tell them you do not expect them to know a lot but that you do expect them to think carefully about the topic.

- When groups are sharing their ideas, ask students to explain their reasoning and support their statements with relevant information they may have or with their own ideas of what seems plausible.

- Encourage debate within and between groups. Ask questions to make students think more deeply about their responses. And don't let students know who's right and who's wrong. Keep them curious!

Speculating can be interesting and energizing for the teacher as well as the students. While you model and promote critical and creative thinking by responding nonjudgmentally to students' ideas, challenging their premises, and making them consider the implications of what they're saying, your own intellect will be stimulated. To help continue such a discussion, keep these kinds of questions and prompts in mind:

- What do you think? Why do you think that?

- Do you all agree or does someone have a different idea?

- Remember: Don't agree (or disagree) just because everyone thinks that way. Think for yourself!

- That's an interesting point. Tell us more about how your thinking led you to that.

- Why have you changed your mind about that?

- What might be a completely different way of looking at this?

- If what you say is true, then that implies _____. Would you say that too?

- Is there something we haven't thought of so far?

- Which of the ideas we're discussing seems the most plausible? the least likely? Why?

When students are ready to read, it's all right for them to read quickly, looking for the points they're most interested in. Sometimes they'll spontaneously take notes or show one another information they're especially interested in. After a first quick read to satisfy curiosity, it's time to reread, review, and reflect on the information in more depth.

After Reading

- Have students say whether the text confirms, qualifies, or refutes their initial hypotheses. Encourage them to cite text statements to support their latest thinking.

- Help students correct misconceptions they may have had before reading.

- Have students state in their own words what they learned. You may want to have them write a paragraph or two about the topic, using statements from the anticipation guide that have been revised or qualified.

- Have students work more actively with the important information from the reading. For instance, you may want them to do additional writing, drawing, constructing, dramatizing, problem-solving, reading, viewing, or discussing to refine and extend key concepts.

The Strategy in Action

Topic: Honoring Women of Achievement

Text: "History Makes Way for Women" (pages 13 to 14)

Other materials: Overhead transparency and individual copies of Monument to the Suffragists Anticipation Guide (page 12)

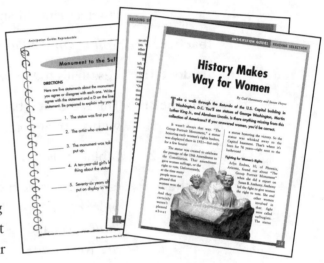

The teacher showed a picture of Susan B. Anthony and said, "Today we'll be learning about a statue that was created as a monument to this woman, Susan B. Anthony, and to other women like her. They fought to give women the right to vote and for this reason were called 'suffragists.' All of these statements have to do with that monument to the suffragists. Decide if you agree or disagree with each one. Put an A or a D in front of each to show what you think. Be prepared to explain your reasoning." The teacher displayed the following statements on an overhead projector.

1. The statue was first put on display in 1921.

2. The artist who created the statue left it unfinished.

3. The monument was taken down as soon as it was put up.

4. A ten-year-old girl's letters forced people to do something about the statue.

5. Seventy-six years after it was made, the statue was put on display in Washington, D.C.

As students worked in small groups to respond to the statements, the teacher circulated to listen in on the discussions, ask probing questions, and encourage students to listen carefully to one another. Then the students were ready for a whole-class discussion. Here's part of the exchange:

Teacher:	*What do you think about statement 1?*
Student 1:	We disagreed with that one. We think the statue was put on display a long time before 1921.
Student 2:	We thought around 1865.
Teacher:	*Why 1865?*
Student 2:	We think that's when women got to vote. That was part of the law that Lincoln signed, wasn't it?
Teacher:	*You mean the Emancipation Proclamation?*
Student 1:	Yes, that's the one.
Student 3:	That's the law that freed the slaves. It didn't have anything to do with women voting, did it?
Student 2:	I think it did.
Teacher:	(after further discussion of statement 1) *We'll have to find out more about that. What about statement 2? How many agreed with that?* (No hands go up.) *So everyone disagrees?* (Heads nod.) *Why are you so sure?*
Student 4:	Because it doesn't make any sense to not finish a whole statue like that!
Student 5:	Especially when it was a monument.
Student 2:	Wait a minute. Maybe the artist was supposed to get paid but he didn't, so he decided not to finish the statue.
Student 4:	Hey, that's a good idea! I think I agree with you. I'm going to change my mind on that one.
Teacher:	*Anyone else?*
Student 6:	Maybe the artist got sick and couldn't finish the statue. That could be another reason he didn't finish it.
Student 7:	Or maybe he died.
Teacher:	(after further discussion of statement 2) *Let's move on to statement 3.*
Student 8:	At first I disagreed with that one because I thought it would be

silly to put a statue up and then take it down right away. But now I'm thinking maybe people noticed it wasn't finished and they didn't like it, so they took it down.

The discussion continued in this way until the group discussed all the statements. The teacher asked probing questions to get students to think from different perspectives and use whatever prior knowledge they had along with their common sense. She didn't give hints about who was correct and who wasn't and didn't try to correct misconceptions, knowing that could all be done after reading. Before long, the students were curious about the statue, and they turned to the text purposefully to find out which of their ideas were correct and which needed to be revised.

Follow-up Activities

The information and concepts in this article can be reinforced with a variety of activities. First, at the end of the lesson, students should review their responses to the anticipation guide, discussing how their thinking was confirmed or how they discovered they were mistaken at first. Next, individuals or small groups can use the new information in various ways and extend their learning beyond the material presented in the text. Here are some ideas of what might be done as follow-up activities for this lesson:

* Have students write skits to dramatize Arlys Endres presenting her ideas before different community groups.

* Have a correspondence team write to their senators or representative in Washington to find out what happened to the statue after the year's display time ended on May 8, 1998.

* Encourage students to gather more information about Susan B. Anthony and other suffragists of the time. Suggest creative ways for them to present their findings to the class.

Monument to the Suffragists

DIRECTIONS

Here are five statements about the monument to suffragists. Decide if you agree or disagree with each one. Write an A on the line if you agree with the statement and a D on the line if you disagree with the statement. Be prepared to explain why you think the way you do.

_____ 1. The statue was first put on display in 1921.

_____ 2. The artist who created the statue left it unfinished.

_____ 3. The monument was taken down as soon as it was put up.

_____ 4. A ten-year-old girl's letters forced people to do something about the statue.

_____ 5. Seventy-six years after it was made, the statue was put on display in Washington, D.C.

History Makes Way for Women

By Gail Hennessey and Susan Hayes

Take a walk through the Rotunda of the U.S. Capitol building in Washington, D.C. You'll see statues of George Washington, Martin Luther King, Jr., and Abraham Lincoln. Is there anything missing from this collection of Americans? If you answered women, you'd be correct.

It wasn't always that way. "The Group Portrait Monument," a statue honoring early women's rights leaders, was displayed there in 1921—but only for a few hours!

The statue was created to celebrate the passage of the 19th Amendment to the Constitution. That amendment gave women suffrage, or the right to vote. Unfortunately, at the time many people were not pleased that women won the vote.

And they certainly weren't pleased about a statue honoring the victory. So the statue was whisked away to the Capitol basement. That's where it's been for 76 years—right next to the bathroom!

Fighting for Women's Rights

Arlys Endres, 10, of Phoenix, Arizona, found out about "The Group Portrait Monument" when she did a report on Susan B. Anthony. Anthony led the fight to give women the right to vote. She and other women involved in that fight were called suffragists. The statue

The Group Portrait Monument

is of Anthony and two other suffragists, Lucretia Mott and Elizabeth Cady Stanton.

The statue's creator, Adelaide Johnson, left the statue unfinished on purpose. "There's a big lump of marble which is supposed to symbolize all the women that come after them who would fight for women's rights," Arlys told *SN*. "One of those fighting is me. If this mound of unfinished marble represents me, I don't want to be in the Capitol basement!"

In the past when someone suggested moving the statue, the answer was always no. There were different reasons: It would cost too much, there wasn't any more room in the Rotunda, it was too heavy, and it wasn't a statue of a President. Still others said it wasn't the best statue to honor women.

A Capitol Rescue

But Arlys wouldn't take no for an answer. She felt a statue honoring Susan B. Anthony would be a great addition to the Rotunda. "I care where the statue is and where it should be. I feel that it's my responsibility to repay Susan B. Anthony for giving me the rights I now have," Arlys told *SN*.

Arlys learned that the Woman Suffrage Statue Campaign needed to raise $75,000 to move the statue.

Arlys began writing letters. She sent nearly 2,000 letters to family, friends, businesses, and politicians. She asked each of them to donate a dollar to help pay for the statue's move. She also gave several speeches. Arlys's letters and speeches earned an impressive $2,000!

Arlys's hard work paid off. On September 27, 1996, Congress passed a bill to move the statue to the Rotunda. It is slated to be moved on May 8—Mother's Day—and will remain there for one year. Arlys is excited about the move, but says there is plenty of work to do. "It doesn't please me that Congress only plans to keep the statue in the Rotunda for one year," she told *SN*. "I want to see that it remains there permanently."

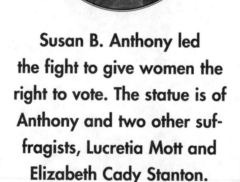

Susan B. Anthony led the fight to give women the right to vote. The statue is of Anthony and two other suffragists, Lucretia Mott and Elizabeth Cady Stanton.

"History Makes Way for Women" originally appeared in Scholastic News, *March 7, 1997.*

Easy Strategies and Mini-Lessons That Build Content Area Reading Skills Scholastic Professional Books, 1999

Facts and Inferences

Strategy Summary

This strategy is used during reading to help students build an awareness of how they process information and understand the differences between facts and inferences. After reading a section of the text, students analyze what they have just read and make a series of statements about the text. Then they categorize the information as either fact or inference, using the text to substantiate their choices. By using this strategy, students monitor their comprehension and learn to read more thoughtfully and purposefully.

Introducing the Strategy

Select an article that contains relatively easy concepts for your students to think about so that they will be able to make some inferences from the facts that are presented. Decide in advance how to divide the piece into four or five segments. Students should be able to read each segment in five or six minutes.

Tell students that you are going to teach them a new strategy that will help them differentiate between facts and inferences. Remind students that an inference is a conclusion derived from facts or information. Then, using the first segment of a story or article, model the following steps.

1. Read the text silently while students read along silently.

2. Tell the class what you remember reading. Record each statement on the board or an overhead transparency. Encourage students to add any information you may have omitted.

3. Then, return to each statement and categorize it as either fact or inference, explaining for each one why you have decided on that category.

4. Return to the text and point out what information led you to the specific categorization.

Guiding the Practice

Tell students they will read the rest of the selection in segments, each time stopping to recall what they have read. Tell them to be prepared to classify the information as fact or inference.

- Have students read the next segment of text, marking the stopping point with a paper clip or book mark.

- When students have finished reading, call their attention to the board or overhead and ask for recall statements. As students give you their recollections, challenge their statements, asking for clarification and having them return to the text to read aloud specific phrases and sentences. Lead them to understand that sometimes what they think is a fact is actually an unexamined assumption, and therefore an inference. Encourage students to add their own comments and assessments of the way the group is categorizing the statements.

- Repeat the steps for each of the other segments of text. At the end of the discussion, have students summarize the difference between a fact and an inference.

Reflecting on the Strategy

When the class has finished reading the full selection, have them discuss in general how they needed to think in order to do the activity. Use questions like these to prompt reflection and self-evaluation:

- What did you find most difficult about this?

- What was relatively easy?

- How can you be sure whether your recollection is a fact or an inference?

- How can this strategy help you when you are reading?

The Strategy in Action

Topic: Animal Helpers

Text: "Animals At Work" (pages 21 to 22)

Other materials: Overhead transparency and individual copies of Fact or Inference? (page 20)

To begin the lesson, the teacher modeled the strategy by reading the first segment silently while students read along with their copies. When she finished, she put her paper down and invited students to do the same when they finished.

Teacher: *These are the things I remember.*

The teacher wrote the following statements on the board.

> Some animals care for people.
>
> Capuchin monkeys are really tiny.
>
> Capuchin monkeys are very easy to train.
>
> Monkeys make disabled persons' lives easier.

Teacher: *I think I got everything.*

Student 1:   It said that people have always depended on animals to do many kinds of jobs.

Teacher: *Oh, right. That was in the beginning of the article. Let's add that to the list. Okay, now let's see if I can tell you which of these statements are facts and which are inferences.*

The teacher categorized the statements as follows while the students watched.

> Fact: Some animals are trained to help disabled people.
>
> Fact: Capuchin monkeys are really tiny.
>
> Fact: Capuchin monkeys are very easy to train.
>
> Inference: Monkeys make disabled persons' lives easier.
>
> Fact: People have always depended on animals to do many kinds of jobs.

Teacher: *Now let's look at my list. I know that the first one is definitely a fact because, as I was reading it, I was thinking that I had seen a television show about this dog who was trained to help a young*

17

	boy. Let's check and see if I am right. (Teacher and students look back at the text.) *Does it say that point right here?*
Student 2:	Yes, it's right here at the end of the second paragraph.
Teacher:	*You're right. And I'm sure that it said the capuchin monkey is tiny.*
Student 3:	No it doesn't. It says that they fit into your backpack.
Teacher:	*Well, what do you know! I know that to fit into a backpack a monkey would have to be pretty small, so I inferred that it is tiny. It doesn't actually say that, does it? Do you agree with the rest of my categories?*
Student 4:	The article says that the monkeys are smart and curious, but it doesn't say that they are easy to train.
Teacher:	*So why do you think I listed that as a fact?*
Student 5:	Well, I guess you thought that if it was really smart and could do all of those things, it must have been easy to train it.
Teacher:	*That's exactly right. It doesn't say anything about them being easy to train. It might take a really long time to train a monkey. Again, I made an inference, only this time I was thinking about the information in the article—words like "smart" and "curious"—and made that inference!*

The class continued to discuss the remaining points and then the teacher had them read the next section on their own. After reading the second section, the class listed their statements and categorized them. The class then discussed what information helped them make inferences.

When they were finished, they discussed how this strategy could help them. Here are two student responses:

Student 6:	Reading this way makes me pay more attention to the article. Sometimes I skip stuff and don't think about what I'm reading. When we do it this way, I have to really think!
Student 5:	I agree with that. Also, I just realized that if you don't read carefully, you can think that it says something when it really doesn't. You have to keep thinking about what the words really say instead of what you think they say.

Follow-up Activities

After students have used the facts and inferences strategy enough so that they're familiar with it, use it regularly in these ways:

✳ Have students work in pairs and share their lists. Have them explain their thinking to their partners. Encourage them to challenge one another and to search the text actively to verify the facts.

✳ Have students try the strategy with different kinds of expository text, such as science or social studies materials, and discuss with which ones they had the easiest (or hardest) time generating inferences.

✳ Have students try the strategy with a piece of fiction that has a particularly strong character. Instead of listing what they recall, discuss the kind of inferences they made based on the description of the character. For example, if the character works as a waitress, do they describe her as working long hours, making little money, having sore feet? Discuss why they made those inferences.

Fact or Inference?

Statements:

Facts: | Inferences:

Animals at Work

By Amanda Agee

Rabbits, cats, dogs, hamsters, snakes, ferrets—there are so many kinds of animals that people love to care for. But did you know that there are also animals who care for people?

Throughout history, humans have depended on animals to perform many kinds of jobs. Animals have guarded homes, herded sheep, hunted food, and pulled plows. Now animals are being trained to help humans in more amazing ways.

Monkey Business

A full-grown capuchin monkey can fit in your backpack. Capuchins are smart, curious, and good at using their hands to pick up and handle objects. This makes them the perfect species to help humans.

For the past 20 years, Dr. Mary Joan Willard has been training capuchin monkeys to help disabled people. At Helping Hands, an organization Willard started in Boston, capuchin monkeys learn to open doors, screw off bottle caps, fetch food from a refrigerator, and even pop a video into a VCR. After graduating from the program, capuchins are placed in homes where they become companions to disabled people.

To their human pals, these monkeys are far more than just helping hands. "She gives me something to think about besides myself," says one disabled teen about his playful capuchin monkey. "Life wouldn't be nearly as much fun without her."

Dogs on Duty

Monkeys aren't the only animals who help humans. Dogs play a special role in the lives of many disabled people. Everyone has heard of Seeing Eye dogs that guide blind people. But have you ever heard of a hearing-ear dog

21

that acts as ears for a deaf person? When an alarm clock rings or a baby cries, these dogs let their owners know, and then lead them to the sound.

Highly trained dogs called "canine companions" help people who can't use their arms or legs. At Canine Companions for Independence in Santa Rosa, California, dogs learn to obey 89 different commands. They can move wheelchairs up walkways, push elevator buttons with their paws, and even carry money to a checkout counter to pay for a purchase!

During accidents or disasters, search-and-rescue dogs can save lives. They use their powerful sense of smell to locate people lost in the wilderness or buried under the rubble of an earthquake or other disaster.

> Animal specialists believe that horses, dogs, and capuchin monkeys are among the animals who just naturally understand the needs of the disabled.

Horse Power

Humans are also training horses to be helpers. There are now special horse-back-riding programs for disabled kids and adults. The horses in these programs know they must stand still while a rider struggles to get in the saddle, stop immediately if a rider falls off, and keep from stepping on a rider who has fallen. Many doctors believe that a kid who learns to sit in a saddle or ride a horse without falling off will be less afraid to try other new things.

Animal specialists believe that horses, dogs, and capuchin monkeys are among the animals who just naturally understand the needs of the disabled. Some people are now asking, "Who understands the needs of the animals?"

How do we know that the animals are happy in their new workplaces? We don't, really. But the people who need these animals love them, feed them, and give them a home and companionship. To them, life wouldn't be the same without the extra pair of helping hands…or hooves or paws.

"Animals at Work" originally appeared in Scholastic News, *November 22, 1996.*

Easy Strategies and Mini-Lessons That Build Content Area Reading Skills Scholastic Professional Books, 1999

Key Words

Strategy Summary

Before reading informational text, students talk about how several key words and terms relate to the topic they are going to read about. As students discuss the words, which come from the selection, they form hypotheses about how the words are connected to the topic. Then students read the material and revise their thinking in light of what they learned from the text. This strategy sparks students' curiosity about the topic, stimulates good thinking, and provides clear purposes for reading. It's easy to use, and fun, too.

Before Reading

- Select anywhere from 5 to 15 words, numbers, or phrases from the text students are going to read. Choose items that can be put together in various ways so that the actual relationships aren't obvious. Make some items purposely ambiguous to stimulate more divergent responses. For instance, instead of using "400 horses," use just "400."

- Have students first work in small groups to speculate on how the terms might relate to the topic, then have them share their thoughts as a whole class. Make sure students know you don't expect them to have the right answers.

- Encourage students to think critically about one another's responses, to explain their reasoning, and to support their hypotheses by citing information they may have or just by telling what makes the most sense to them.

- To keep students curious and motivated to read, don't give away the answers. Focus on the quality of their reasoning rather than the accuracy of their statements. Don't call attention to misconceptions, which you can address after they've read the text.

When students are ready to read, you may want to have them take notes or mark where the key terms appear in the text. It's all right for them to read quickly at first to find the things they are most interested in. You can take time after reading to review and reflect on the information in more depth.

After Reading

- Have students discuss each term, citing text information to show they now understand how the term relates to the topic.

- Bring up and discuss any misconceptions students may have revealed before reading. Reread the text and discuss these points to clarify and develop meanings.

- Have students restate what they learned, either orally or in writing or both. You may want to have them write a paragraph or two about the topic, using all the key words in the initial display.

- Challenge students to apply the important information, for instance by using it to create question-answer games that they can play to review the information and test their recall of it.

This strategy calls for you to interact with students in much the same way that the anticipation guides do. The key is to encourage speculation and reduce their concern about having the right answer. It's important to respond neutrally to whatever students say, whether they are voicing what you know to be incorrect information or stating the correct facts. These kinds of questions help keep the sharing of ideas free from undue concern about being right:

- What do you think that term has to do with the topic? Why do you think that?

- Do you all agree, or has someone thought of a different possible connection?

- That's an interesting connection. What was the train of thought that led to that idea?

- Explain why you've changed your mind on that point.

- Which of the ideas we're discussing seems the most plausible? the least? Why?

The Strategy in Action

Topic: Child Labor

Text: "The Cost of Child Labor" (pages 29 to 31)

Other material: Overhead transparency of Key Words: Child Labor (page 28)

At the start of the lesson, the teacher put this array on the overhead projector and said, "Today we will be learning something about child labor. All of these terms have something to do with child labor. What do you think the connections are?"

CHILD LABOR

soccer	250 million	60 cents
$6.00		Pakistan
$30.00	New York	rugs

Students broke into groups to discuss their ideas, and the teacher circulated to ask questions and encourage students to listen and respond to each other. Then each group shared their thinking with the whole class. Here's part of that exchange:

Teacher: *What connections do you think these words have with child labor?*

Student 1: Our group is pretty sure that kids somewhere make soccer balls. A couple of us saw something about that on TV once. We think maybe they did it in Pakistan. And we think they sit on rugs on the floor when they make the balls.

Student 2: We agree with that, except about the rugs. We think they have to sleep in the factory and they sleep on rugs at night. We think

25

that would be awful. We also think they get six dollars a day for making the balls.

Teacher: *Why do you think six dollars a day makes sense as a wage?*

Student 2: Well, we figured grownups here make over six dollars an hour, and the kids that make those balls make a lot less than people do here, and they're kids, too, so they wouldn't make a whole lot, so that's why we think it's six dollars a day.

Teacher: *What do others think?*

Student 3: We agree that the kids make soccer balls, but we don't think they make six dollars a day. That isn't enough to live on! We think they get six dollars for every ball they make.

Teacher: *So how many balls do you think a child could make in a day?*

Student 3: Hmmm. Probably four or five. Maybe more.

Teacher: *So how much would that child make a day, then, if you're right about six dollars a ball?*

Student 4: Well, that would be 6 times 4, so 24 dollars. Or $30 if they can make five balls a day. That doesn't sound like much money, though. Maybe they make more balls than that.

Teacher: *Anyone else?*

Student 5: I think they just hardly make any money at all. They're like slaves almost. So I think they make 60 cents for every ball they make.

Teacher: *Then what do you think six dollars has to do with this?*

Student 5: Maybe that's what they make in a month. Or maybe a week or two weeks or something like that.

Teacher: *Any ideas abut the other terms?*

Student 6: We think the factory sends the soccer balls that the kids make to New York, and then they get sent to stores like the one where I bought mine. I think $30 is what a soccer ball costs here because that's about what I paid for mine.

The discussion continued in this way until the group had addressed all the terms. Some students changed their initial thinking because of points others raised, while others stayed with their first responses. The teacher continued asking questions to probe their thinking more deeply and encouraged them to question each other as well. Although the teacher knew the students were right about some of the terms, he did not tell them that, wanting instead for them to find out for themselves by reading the material. When they finished reading, he had them write about the topic for five minutes, without looking at the text, using as many of the key words as possible. Students then read their writings to each other and finally composed a group summary, with the help of the teacher. The teacher recorded this on a transparency and made copies of the summary for the children to add to their notes.

Follow-up Activities

After students have reviewed and discussed the information in the reading material, it's usually a good idea to reinforce and extend learning by having them complete one or more related activities. Here are some follow-up activities that would be appropriate for this lesson:

* Have students search the Internet or available print materials for up-to-date information on child labor issues. For instance, students might look for a more recent UNICEF report on children of the world than the one cited in the article ("The State of the World's Children 1997").

* Challenge students to research information about Pakistan and other developing countries to find out more about their standards of living and current positions regarding child labor.

* Have students search print periodicals or Internet locations to find out the latest about the reliance on child labor by the U.S. manufacturers mentioned in the article (Adidas, Nike, Reebok).

* Encourage students to write letters to the editor that express their concern about child labor, citing information in the article to make key points. Completed letters can be sent to the local newspaper or published in the school newspaper.

Child Labor

soccer   250 million   60 cents

$6.00   Pakistan

$30.00   New York   rugs

The Cost of Child Labor

By Susan Hayes

Millions of children go to work instead of school. Will the world change the way they spend their days? Can you imagine what it would be like if you didn't have to go to school? No more homework, no more tests, no more teachers.

Sounds great, right? But what if not going to school meant going to work to help support your family? And what if it meant you spent your day breaking up stones into gravel; or harvesting tobacco; or making rugs or soccer balls in a dark, dirty place for a few pennies an hour? In many countries around the world, this is how children your age spend their days.

Almost every country in the world has laws that forbid adults to employ children. But in the fall of 1996, the International Labor Organization (ILO) said that 250 million 5- to 14-year-olds work in Asia, Africa, and Central and South America. Half of them work full-time. Millions of them have never been to school at all.

This very high number prompted the world to take action. Public pressure is forcing businesses to promise that their products are not made by child labor. Organizations like the ILO and UNICEF are studying the problem and recommending solutions.

Stitching Soccer Balls, Weaving Rugs

Why are so many children forced to work? In some countries like India and Pakistan, very poor parents sell their children to factory owners. These children are called bonded workers, but they are practically slaves. They must work for the factory owner until they pay back the money that was given to their parents. Because the children earn so little money, this takes years and

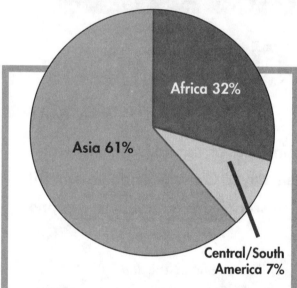

Africa 32%

Asia 61%

Central/South
America 7%

Where Children Work

Child labor exists in almost every country in the world. But the vast majority of working children—about 250 million—live in Asia, Africa, and Central and South America. They are between the ages of 5 and 14. The graph shows the percentage of this young workforce that is employed in each of these regions.

years. They work in terrible conditions. Many become sick and die before they become adults. Factory owners want child workers for jobs like stitching soccer balls or weaving rugs. They say it's because children have small, quick fingers. But many people believe the real reason is that children can be ordered around more easily than adults. And they don't have to be paid as much. "For what I'd pay one second-class adult weaver I can get three boys, sometimes four, who produce first-class rugs in no time," one rug maker in Pakistan said.

Each year thousands of Pakistani children sew together pieces of leather to make soccer balls. They earn 60 cents on average for each ball. It takes a whole day to make two balls. Factory owners then sell the finished balls to sporting-goods companies for about $6 each. The companies sell the balls in countries like the U.S. for $30 to $50.

Hopefully, that will soon change, thanks in part to letters and petitions signed by thousands of soccer-playing kids and their parents. Public outrage led the ILO, UNICEF, soccer-ball manufacturers like Adidas, Nike, and Reebok, and a business organization in Pakistan to make an announcement. Last month, they said they would work together to end child labor in the soccer-ball industry in Pakistan within the next 18 months. They set up a $1 million fund to pay for a program that will be run by the

Easy Strategies and Mini-Lessons That Build Content Area Reading Skills Scholastic Professional Books, 1999

How One Boy Works to Free Children

Many people think Craig Kielburger is the most powerful kid in the world. Two years ago, when he was 12, Craig started a group called Free the Children. The group's purpose is to end child labor. Craig has traveled to Asia and South America to make people aware of child labor there.

Craig started Free the Children in 1995 after reading a newspaper article about a Pakistani boy named Iqbal Masih. When Iqbal was 4, his parents sold him to a carpet-maker. Iqbal spent six years tied to a rug loom before he escaped.

Iqbal won the world's attention by speaking out against child labor. Then, when he was 12, Iqbal was shot and killed. Many people think he was killed by local rug merchants. Craig says he started Free the Children to take up Iqbal's mission. "Kids can make a difference," he says.

ILO. The program will pay to send the child workers to school. Inspectors will make sure children aren't working at the ball-making sites.

Child Labor in the U.S.

Americans are horrified by stories of child labor in other countries, but many don't realize it exists in the United States, too. According to the National Child Labor Committee (NCLC) in New York City, close to 500,000 children under the age of 14 work in fields or factories in the United States. "Farm owners hire and pay adult workers to harvest their fruits and vegetables. But many of the owners expect the workers' children to help out too," NCLC presi-dent Jeffrey Newman told SN. "Thousands of 9-, 10-, and 11-year-old children work eight hours a day in the fields, in addition to going to school. And they either get paid very little or they don't get paid at all."

Thousands more children work in clothing factories in cities like New York and Los Angeles.

The good news is that the world is finally talking about child labor. But one thing is sure: As UNICEF says in its recent report on child labor, The State of the World's Children 1997, "The lives of working children will not change unless the world backs its words with action."

"The Cost of Child Labor" originally appeared in Scholastic News, *March 21, 1997.*

Easy Strategies and Mini-Lessons That Build Content Area Reading Skills Scholastic Professional Books, 1999

Key Words II

Strategy Summary

Before reading informational text, students categorize key words and terms by speculating on whether the items are related to the topic or not. The hypotheses they form become their purposes for reading. After they read the material, they discuss their original responses, and revise as needed. This is a variation on the basic key word strategy and is used for the same purposes: to arouse students' curiosity about the topic, to stimulate good thinking, and to provide clear purposes for reading. This variation can be used at any grade level, but it's especially appropriate in the lower grades or with older children who are having difficulty reading.

Before Reading

- Select 5 to 10 words, numbers, or phrases from the article students are going to read. Choose items that can be put together plausibly in various ways. If possible, choose some words that might not immediately be associated with the topic because they have different meanings in other contexts. To this list, add three or four items that do not appear in the text and that are not related to the topic but that seem to belong in the group. The overall purpose here is to construct a set of terms that will provoke thinking but that will not give away the correct answers.

- If you want students to work in small groups, make a set of word cards for each group with one key word printed on each card. If you want to do this as a whole-class activity, copy the words on an overhead transparency. Then cut the words out into small cards that you can arrange on an overhead projector. Another alternative is to make one set of large cards that can be placed in a card holder or taped to the board.

- If you think students will not be able to read some of the words, take a few minutes to pronounce each word for them as they look at the word in print. For instance, put the words on the board, one at a time, pronounce them, and have students find that word in their card sets. Don't explain what the words have to do with the topic, though, as this would defeat the purpose of the activity.

- Have students speculate on which terms relate to the topic and which do not, arranging the cards in two sets to show what they think. If students are working in small groups, have the groups share their ideas with the rest of the class. Assure students that you do not expect them to have the correct answers but that you are interested in what they think and why.

- Encourage students to explain their reasoning, to think critically about one another's responses, and to support their responses by relating what they may already know about the topic or just by saying what they think is plausible. (See the previous section, Key Words, for suggestions of questions to pose and tips on conducting the discussion.)

- Ask questions to make students think more deeply about their responses, but avoid giving hints that would prompt the correct answers. Give neutral responses—such as "Hmmm" or "I see" or "That's an interesting idea"—to keep them thinking and interested.

Once students have discussed their ideas and are curious, have them turn to the text and read in order to learn more. You may want to have students who have difficulty reading scan the text for the key words rather than try to read every word. When they find words, you can read that part with them and discuss the meaning of the sentences. Or you may want to read the text aloud as they read along, in which case you can stop to discuss points as they notice the key words. However you handle this step, the important goal is for students to turn to the text with a clear purpose in mind and find the information they are seeking.

After Reading

- Ask students to look again at their cards and rearrange them, stating what they learned. If students had any misconceptions about the topic, clear those up by rereading with them and discussing those points in detail.

- Invite students to draw or write what they learned, using the key words that relate to the topic. For instance, they might draw pictures and use the words as labels. Or each one can write about the topic, using one or more of the key words, and then read their accounts aloud to the whole class.

This version of the key word strategy is especially appropriate for students with limited reading abilities because the format of the word-sort task is relatively easy, involving a simple yes-no decision. Because of this, they can devote their attention to thinking about the terms. Also, poorer readers can feel a sense of accomplishment by simply finding some of the words in the text and thus confirming that those words have something to do with the topic. For students with good reading abilities, the format of the activity can provide an interesting change of pace from the regular key word strategy.

The Strategy in Action

Topic: Climbing Mount Everest

Text: "Mount Everest: The Ultimate Challenge" (pages 39 to 40)

Other materials: A set of Climbing Mount Everest Word Cards (page 38) for each group of students

At the start of the lesson, the teacher wrote Mount Everest on the board, organized students into groups, gave each group a set of note cards, and said, "Today we will be learning something about climbing the tallest mountain in the world, Mount Everest. Some of these terms have something to do with that, and some of them don't. Which ones do you think are "Mount Everest words," and which ones do you think are not?"

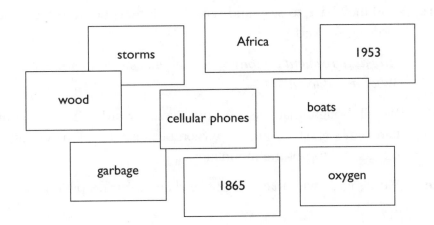

Students worked together to discuss what they thought and to categorize the cards into two piles. The teacher circulated to monitor discussions, ask probing questions, and encourage students to listen and respond to each other. Then she had small groups share their ideas as a whole class. Here's part of that discussion:

Teacher: *What did you decide about Africa?*

Student 1:   We didn't know what to do with that one. Some of us think Mount Everest is in Africa and some of us don't. Who's right?

Teacher: *Those of you who think Mount Everest is in Africa, why do you think so?*

Student 2:   I saw a TV program about Africa last year, and there's this really big mountain there, and I remember they said it was Mount Everest.

Student 3:   I disagree. My dad's a climber, and he told me about Mount Everest, and he said it's in China, or some place close to China. And he knows what he's talking about!

Teacher: *Anyone else have any ideas?*

Student 4:   I think Mount Everest is in Africa, too. I remember seeing a picture of it! *(Others offer equally strong opinions.)*

Teacher: (laughing) *Well, everyone seems pretty sure about what they think, so I don't suppose any of you are going to change your mind! Let's discuss another term. What about storms?*

Student 5:   We thought that was definitely a yes word because when you see pictures of mountain climbers, a lot of times the snow is blowing all over . . .

35

Student 1: And they have to stop and stay in their tents because the wind is blowing so hard.

Teacher: *Any disagreement on that one?* (Students shake their heads.) *What about the word "oxygen"?*

Student 4: We all thought that was a Mount Everest word. We think mountain climbers have to carry oxygen because there isn't enough oxygen on top of the mountains.

Student 5: We disagree with that. We put oxygen in our no pile.

Teacher: *Why?*

Student 5: We just didn't think it had anything to do with mountain climbing.

Student 1: I didn't think so either, but, you know, they do have to have oxygen when they're climbing. I mean, everyone has to have oxygen to do anything!

Teacher: *Do you think there's less oxygen as they go up the mountain?*

Student 1: I don't know...

Student 3: That doesn't make any sense. There's oxygen everywhere, isn't there? I mean, there are animals that live way up on mountains, and they have to have oxygen, so there has to be some up there.

Student 4: Yeah, there's some, but there's not enough for the climbers, so they carry oxygen tanks. I know that, but I don't know why there isn't enough up there.

The teacher kept the discussion going until the group had addressed all the terms and each group had reported their thinking. She welcomed differences of opinion and encouraged debate, knowing that this would raise their curiosity. She also knew that, because many students were wrong about much of what they said, they would have to change their thinking quite a lot after reading. When they finally turned to the article, the exclamations of surprise ("I didn't know that!" or "I can't believe we were wrong about that one!") showed clearly that students were correcting their own misconceptions. When all had finished reading, the teacher had them each write about the topic for five minutes, without looking back at the text, using as many of the key words as possible. Next, students reread the article, correcting any factual errors in their written notes, and then read their writings to each other. Finally, they composed a group summary, with the help of the teacher. She recorded this on a transparency and later photocopied it for the children to add to their notes.

Follow-up Activities

Discussing and writing about the information may be enough to bring closure to the lesson, but additional postreading activities can reinforce and extend learning in interesting ways. Here are some follow-up activities that would be appropriate for this lesson:

❋ Have students search the Internet or print libraries for up-to-date information about attempts to climb Mount Everest, then display what they find in posters or charts. Or they could publish the information in an illustrated bulletin called "Climbing Mount Everest."

❋ Invite students to research the kinds of supplies a mountain climber must have to meet the challenge of Mount Everest. Besides using books, magazines, and Internet sites as sources of information, they might also interview local climbers or clerks at stores that cater to climbers.

❋ Challenge students to learn more about what it's like to live at high altitudes and what effects high altitudes have on people who are used to living at sea level.

❋ Have students make a chart that compares the different heights of the major mountains mentioned in the sidebar.

Climbing Mount Everest

Africa	storms	garbage
1953	boats	1865
wood	cellular phones	oxygen

Mount Everest: The Ultimate Challenge

The peak of Mount Everest, the highest spot on Earth, used to be a tough place to get to. The mountain is set deep in the Himalaya, on the border of Nepal and China. For centuries, only the heartiest of souls could even reach the mountain, let alone climb it.

In 1953, Sir Edmund Hillary and his guide, Tenzing Norgay, became the first people to scale all 29,028 feet of Everest. Since then, more than 4,000 people have tried to reach its peak. Many climbers have come away with an incredible experience. They also have contributed $90 million to Nepal's struggling economy. But some people say that Everest is too dangerous—and its environment is too fragile—for this kind of heavy traffic.

Modern technology, such as e-mail and cellular phones, now makes it easier for climbers to communicate with faraway people—including rescue squads. The number of businesses that take amateur climbers to

39

the summit of Everest has grown too. Critics say that these advantages allow too many inexperienced climbers to attempt Everest's treacherous terrain. About 1 in every 30 Everest climbers dies in the attempt.

The perils of Everest became especially clear in May 1996. Thirty-one people were on the summit when a sudden storm blew up. The wind-chill was minus 140° Fahrenheit, and hurricane-

Highest Mountains
(by continent)

Asia *Mount Everest, Nepal-China border*	29,028 ft.
South America *Mount Aconcagua, Argentina*	22,834 ft.
North America *Mount McKinley, U.S. (Alaska)*	20,230 ft.
Africa *Mount Kilimanjaro, Tanzania*	19,340 ft.
Oceania *Mount Jaja, New Guinea*	16,500 ft.
Europe *Mont Blanc, France-Italy border*	15,771 ft.

force winds blew sheets of snow. The climbers struggled back to their camp, but their oxygen supply dwindled. Eight of them died.

The increasing number of climbers is harming the mountain's fragile environment. Climbers use up valuable resources, such as wood, at a faster rate than the local people. Exhausted, air-starved climbers also leave behind oxygen cylinders, food remains, and other garbage. At that high altitude, land is delicate—toilet paper can take 30 years to decompose. Everest has been called the world's highest dump.

Despite these problems, Everest remains the ultimate challenge to climbers. Some people hope, though, that the May disaster will make some climbers rethink their attitudes. "I have a feeling that people have been getting just a little bit too casual with Mount Everest," says Sir Edmund Hillary. "[Incidents like these] will bring them to regard it rather more seriously."

"Mount Everest: The Ultimate Challenge"
originally appeared in Junior Scholastic, *November 15, 1996.*

Easy Strategies and Mini-Lessons That Build Content Area Reading Skills Scholastic Professional Books, 1999

List • Group • Label

Strategy Summary

List•Group•Label is a before-reading strategy in which students examine a list of words taken from a text, look for relationships among words, group the words tentatively, and identify the unifying concept for the groupings they create. Through the discussion and manipulation of the words, students are better prepared to read the text as they have become familiar with the words and have thought about the possible relationships among them. This strategy helps students access background knowledge, stimulates their thinking, and prepares them to read purposefully.

Before Reading

● Select 25 to 30 words from the selection. The words should be essential to understanding the main idea of the text. Do not select more than 30, or students may feel overwhelmed. When selecting the words, make sure that they can be grouped into categories. Also, choose one or two words that don't fit easily into obvious categories. Adding these words will challenge the students' thinking about categories.

● Give students the list of words. Ask students to identify which words on the list are familiar to them. As you go through the list, pronounce each word for the students so that they know how to say it even if they're not familiar with the concept.

- If some words are unfamiliar to students, ask them to speculate about the meanings and explain what clues they're using to figure out the meanings. Have they ever seen the word before? Does the word sound familiar? Are there any other clues? For example, if the word is capitalized, it might be the name of a person or a town.

- Divide students into pairs or allow them to work individually. Have students group the words into categories and think about what the overall topic might be. Tell them that each word in the list should be in a group. If they are not sure which group a word belongs to, they should make their best guess. Remind them that they are forming hypotheses, not trying to figure out right answers, and that after reading they will have an opportunity to rearrange their lists. Encourage students to discuss their reasons for putting words in a particular group and to challenge their own thinking. Ask them to think of more than one way to group the words.

- After students have categorized the words, have them create labels for each category. They may give each group a title or explain how the words in the group are related.

- When students have finished grouping and labeling the words, have them share their list with another pair or with the class. Encourage them to explain their rationale for the categories and labels. Then have them speculate on what they think the overall topic is.

- Have students read the material to check their hypotheses.

After Reading

- Have students rearrange their lists based on the information they have just read. They may also want to change the labels or rethink their rationale for grouping. Allow them ample time to discuss why they are changing their lists or labels.

- Allow students time to discuss any misconceptions they had initially. Have them locate the parts of the text that helped them correct their misconceptions.

- Have students write a summary of the text, using the words from their lists. They may want to use the labels as organizers.

Allowing students ample time for discussion and hypothesizing is critical with this strategy. Encourage them to challenge their own ideas as well as each other's ideas. As you circulate around the room, ask questions such as, "Why do these seem to go together? What other label could you use? Are there other words that could be included in this list that you have placed in another category?"

The Strategy in Action

Topic: Hijacking a Train

Text: "Hijacked!" (pages 47 to 49)

Other materials: Copies of the List•Group•Label Word list (page 46)

To begin the lesson, the teacher had the students select partners and then distributed the following list.

Civil War	Union
Chattanooga	Confederate
commandeered	stolen
railroads	passenger cars
gallows	boxcars
telegraph lines	pursuit
communications	90 miles
supply	prisoners
wrecked	throttle
conductor	civilian
volunteered	soldiers
Medal of Honor	captured
hanged	General
Texas	locomotive

The pairs grouped the words into categories and then labeled each category. The teacher circulated around the room, asking questions and encouraging students to create even more categories. Then several groups shared their categories and labels with the whole class. Here's part of that exchange.

Teacher: *I noticed that your group started putting words together right away. What did you start with?*

Student 1: When we looked at the list, the first word was Civil War, so we decided to look for words that had to do with war and we found a lot of them. We grouped "soldier," "Civil War," "confederate," "Union," "volunteer," "Medal of Honor," and "civilian" together.

Teacher: *Okay, and what was the label for that group?*

Student 1: "War."

Teacher: *Anyone have any questions about their War category?*

Student 2: Yes, I do! Why would you put the word "civilian" in a war category?

Student 1: Because even during a war there are people who aren't fighting the war and they are called civilians.

Teacher: (to Student 2) *Do you agree with them?*

Student 2: Yeah, that makes sense, but we put "civilian" in another category.

Teacher: *What was that?*

Student 2: Well, we put "civilian" with "conductor" and called that group "People who are on a train."

Teacher: *Okay. What words on the list were difficult to categorize?*

Student 4: We couldn't figure out a place for "90 miles." We finally put it with "telegraph lines" and "communication" and labeled it "Old Ways to Keep in Touch."

Teacher: *Interesting label! But explain how "90 miles" fits in there.*

Student 5: We figured that towns had to be at least 90 miles apart for them to put in telegraph lines. And communication goes in that category because that's what telegraphs are for.

Teacher: *Anyone place "90 miles" in another category?*

Student 6: We put it in our grouped labeled "Outlaws" along with "pursuit," "commandeered," "captured," "prisoners," "hanged" and "stole." We figured it fit there because they probably chased these outlaws at least 90 miles before they finally caught them.

Student 7: I think 90 miles was really far to go in the olden days. It would take a really long time to go 90 miles on a horse.

Student 6:   Yeah, but we don't think they were on horses. We just figured they were on a train. We had "conductor" in that category too. And we thought the good guys might be chasing them in another train.

Student 7:   Where would they get another train? It's not like they just have trains sitting around that they can go chase another train.

The discussion continued until the students had an opportunity to discuss all the categories they had created and the rationale for each. The teacher encouraged the students to challenge each other's thinking. The teacher was able to learn about the students' knowledge of the Civil War and their misconceptions. After the discussion went on for a while, the students started asking the teacher when they could read the article because they wanted to know if they had grouped the words as they were in the story. As the students read, there were many comments ("Hey, they did go 90 miles!" and "The civilian was part of the gang and a passenger on the train!").

When the class finished reading, the teacher had each pair go back to their original papers and regroup and relabel based on the information in the article. Next, students individually wrote short summaries of the article and read them to each other. Finally, the group listed what they had learned on the board and what questions they still had about the train hijacking and the Civil War.

Follow-up Activities

Many times the activities described above are enough to bring closure to the lesson, but sometimes students become so curious that they want to continue finding out more information and doing some research on their own. Here are some follow-up activities that would be appropriate for this lesson:

* Ask students to check the Internet to see if there were any more unusual battles during the Civil War and to find out the impact they may have had on the outcome.

* Invite students to research the heroes of the Civil War. Who were they and what were their contributions?

* Encourage students to find out more about train travel in the United States. They can also investigate whether or not trains are still being used to ship military supplies.

* Challenge students to compare the time it would take to travel 90 miles by train, by car, and by horse. Have them present the information on a chart.

45

List•Group•Label Word List

Civil War	Union
Chattanooga	Confederate
commandeered	stolen
railroads	passenger cars
gallows	boxcars
telegraph lines	pursuit
communications	90 miles
supply	prisoners
wrecked	throttle
conductor	civilian
volunteered	soldiers
Medal of Honor	captured
hanged	General
Texas	locomotive

HIJACKED!

A famous train hijacking showed the importance of railroads in the Civil War

By Michael Cusack

The U.S. Civil War (1861-1865) has been called the first modern war. It saw the first use of machine guns, repeating rifles, long-range artillery, and observation balloons. It also saw the first battle between iron gunboats and the first destruction of a warship by a submarine. But none of those new weapons played a large role in the war.

Most of the rifles and cannons on both sides were old-fashioned muzzle-loaders (guns that soldiers loaded by ramming gunpowder and bullets down the barrel). Military leaders on both sides resisted the use of machine guns because, they said, they wasted ammunition. Most warships were wooden. The battle between iron gunboats ended in a standoff, and the submarine that sank the warship destroyed itself.

Two technological advances did play a big role in the war: railroads and telegraph lines. In both the Union and the Confederate states, the railroads were like arteries carrying the lifeblood of supplies and troops to far-flung battlefronts. The electric telegraph wires were like nerves flashing vital messages over great distances. Those lines of supply and communications were so important that both sides made great efforts to protect their own and to smash those of the enemy.

A Wild Plan

In March 1862, Union troops near Nashville,

Easy Strategies and Mini-Lessons That Build Content Area Reading Skills Scholastic Professional Books, 1999

Tennessee, were ordered to capture Chattanooga. But a large, well-supplied Confederate force stood in their way.

James J. Andrews, a Union Army spy, had a wild idea. He offered to lead a band of soldiers in civilian clothes to Marietta, Georgia, more than 200 miles away. There, they would hijack a Confederate train and head north. Along the way, they would rip up rails, burn bridges, and cut telegraph lines. With Confederate supply and communication lines wrecked, Union troops could then attack Chattanooga.

Andrews explained his plan to General Ormsby MacKnight Mitchel, who gave the go-ahead. Andrews asked for volunteers—especially men with railroad experience. He warned them that they risked being killed if they got captured. Even so, 22 soldiers and 1 civilian volunteered.

The raiders set out on the night of April 7, 1861, in a rainstorm. They planned to meet in Marietta, Georgia, on April 11. The next day, they would get on the early-morning train from Atlanta to Chattanooga. When the train stopped for breakfast at Big Shanty, eight miles north of Marietta, they would seize it.

Corporal Daniel Dorsey wrote: It was narrowly daylight when we boarded the northbound train at Marietta, 20 miles north of Atlanta, 118 miles south from Chattanooga, and more than 200 miles from General Mitchel...We took seats in the cars in sleepy, drowsy manner. The conductor took our fares...and asked no questions."

The Hijacking

As the train pulled into Big Shanty station, the conductor, William A. Fuller, shouted, "Twenty minutes for breakfast." The passengers and train crew rushed to the restaurant. Andrews and his raiders pretended to go to, but circled around the train instead. Privates Wilson Brown, Bill Knight, and Alf Wilson—all engineers—jumped on the locomotive. It was the *General*, which had been built in Paterson, New Jersey.

Andrews disconnected the passenger cars, leaving three boxcars behind the locomotive. The other raiders scrambled into the boxcars. The men in the locomotive's cab released the brake and opened the throttle. They were off.

The hiss of escaping steam made Fuller, Cain, and Murphy jump up from their breakfast. The *General*'s conductor, engineer, and railroad foreman rushed to the door just in time to see their locomotive and three boxcars racing away. Someone had stolen their train!

At first, everything went according to plan for the raiders. By quickly cutting the telegraph line, they prevented Fuller from alerting Marietta, Atlanta, or other stations along the northward line.

The Chase

Fuller sent a horseman to Marietta to spread the word that a train had been hijacked. Then he, Cain, and Murphy set out in pursuit on a handcar (a small,

Easy Strategies and Mini-Lessons That Build Content Area Reading Skills Scholastic Professional Books, 1999

open railroad car powered by a hand pump). They pumped furiously for several miles. Just as their strength was giving out, they found a mining company locomotive parked on a side-track. They fired it up, and set out after the *General*.

Meanwhile, it was slow going for Andrews and his raiders. They had to bluff their way past Confederate officials at some stations. They had to make way for other trains. They also took time out to rip up rails and cut wires. Their attempts to burn bridges failed because of heavy rain.

Unknown to the raiders, Fuller and the other Confederate pursuers had commandeered the *Texas*, an express train from Rome, Georgia. They took off in hot pursuit after the *General*.

The Capture

The *General* had traveled almost 90 miles since it was hijacked. But it was running out of the wood that it burned for fuel. The raiders edged slowly along, hoping to find a stack of cut logs. Then they spotted a plume of smoke behind them. Soon they could see the *Texas* racing toward them.

To lighten their load, the raiders cut the boxcars loose. Then they set fire to a bridge. But the Texas kept coming. To add to their problems, Confederate cavalry could be seen ahead.

The raiders put the *General* in reverse, sending it back toward the Texas. Then they jumped off and ran for the woods. The *Texas* was able to stop in time, and the *General* ran out of steam. There was no collision.

Within hours, all the raiders were captured. Andrews and seven others were sentenced to death. Andrews escaped but was recaptured. The prisoners were sent to Atlanta. On June 7, 1862, Andrews was hanged. Eleven days later, seven of his fellow raiders went to the gallows. One of them hushed the jeering crown with these words: "The seven of us have been condemned here as spies. We aren't that... We came in performance of our duty as soldiers. A lot of you are going to live to be sorry for what you're doing. More than that you're going to see the Stars and Stripes waving again over the ground this gallows stands on."

Mixed Results

As a result of the raid, the Confederates pulled troops back to protect their communication lines. But not until August 1863, nearly a year after the hijacking, did Union forces capture Chattanooga. The executed raider's last words came true on September 2, 1864, when the Stars and Stripes was raised over Atlanta.

The soldiers in Andrews' raid became the first winners of the Congressional Medal of Honor, the highest U.S. award for bravery. James J. Andrews became a folk hero—the subject of books, songs, and movies.

"Hijacked" originally appeared in Junior Scholastic, *January 24, 1997.*

News Flash

Strategy Summary

News Flash is a strategy that is used during reading to summarize important ideas. The summary, in sentence form, must be exactly 20 words. Students read several paragraphs and stop to summarize what they have read in twenty words. Then they read several more paragraphs and revise their summary to incorporate additional important ideas. This strategy allows students to focus on key information and evaluate the relative importance of the various points. Students also have a clear purpose and enhanced motivation for reading.

Before Reading

- Select a nonfiction article, one that is clear and well-written and that you think is suitable for the whole class. (It's best to do this as a whole-class activity several times before having students try this individually or in pairs.)

- Tell students that they will be reading just a short section of the piece and then summarizing the important ideas. Explain that you will not be writing down every detail, just the important ones. Suggest that the group write the summary so that it sounds like a "news flash" on television.

- Draw 20 short lines on the board to use for recording the 20 words of the summary. Either four rows of five lines or five rows of four lines will work well. You can also use an overhead transparency for this activity. (See News Flash! on page 54.)

During Reading

- To start, have students read a short segment of the piece—no more than three or four paragraphs.

- Begin by asking for the most important facts from the paragraphs they have just read. You may want to jot these down on the board as they give them to you. As they are discussing the key points, you can cross out the ones they decide are not as important.

- After they have had ample time to discuss the important facts, ask a volunteer to try to summarize the article in sentence form. As the student is talking, write the summary on the 20 lines you have put on the board, one word per line. Allow students opportunities to change words and edit ideas. Using the chalkboard will give you the flexibility to revise easily.

- After students are satisfied with the summary, have them read several more paragraphs. The information from these paragraphs must now be incorporated into the existing 20-word summary. Again, have students discuss the important ideas as you jot them on the board. Ask for a volunteer to revise the existing summary by incorporating the new ideas.

- After the summary has been revised several times, students should finish the rest of the article and do one last summary.

With this strategy, students begin to evaluate the relative significance of ideas and concepts. The important thing is to allow them to challenge and revise one another's summaries. If you use a larger selection, you can extend the summary to 30 words.

The Strategy in Action

Topic: Jackie Robinson

Text: "A Major League Hero" (pages 55 to 56)

Other materials: Copies of News Flash! Summary (page 54)

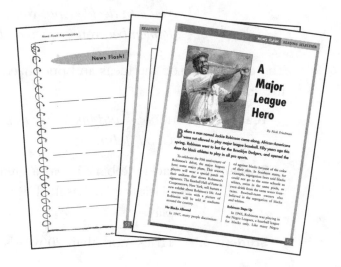

At the start of the lesson the teacher drew 20 lines on the board and said, "Today we are going to read an article about Jackie Robinson. We are going to read several paragraphs and then write a 20 word summary. Then, we will read several more paragraphs and revise our 20 word summary. Let's get started."

Students read the first two paragraphs of the article. Then they discussed the important facts. Here is part of that discussion:

Teacher:	*What are the important facts in these first two paragraphs?*
Student 1:	Well, I think it's important that Jackie Robinson was the first black athlete to play in the major leagues.
Teacher:	*Okay, let's jot that on the board. What else?*
Student 2:	They are going to sell a coin that has his picture on it.
Student 3:	I don't think that's as important as the fact that because he was allowed to play, other blacks were allowed to play.
Student 2:	Well, why can't we put all the ideas up there and then decide.
Teacher:	*Good suggestion. Let's add that to the list and then prioritize our list. What other ideas are important?*
Student 4:	I think it's important that it's the 50th anniversary.
Student 5:	And that the players are going to wear a special patch on their uniform.
Teacher:	*Okay, anything else?*
Student 3:	The Baseball Hall of Fame is going to have a special exhibit about him.
Teacher:	*Great. Anything else? No, well then let's look at the list and see if you can decide what you want to include in the summary. Remember, you have to do this in just 20 words.*

The class discussed the ideas and prioritized them. Then the teacher had them create the summary.

Teacher:	*Who would like to try to put all these ideas into 20 words? Good, John.*
Student 5:	Jackie Robinson was a great baseball player. He was the first black to play baseball. Because of him other black players could play.
Student 6:	That's more than 20 words, and we haven't got all the big ideas.

Teacher: *Okay, how should we change this? Any suggestions?*

Student 6:   I think we should take out "was a great baseball player" and say "Jackie Robinson was the first black athlete to play baseball."

Student 7:   Then we could add: "This is the 50th anniversary. There are many things planned to celebrate."

Teacher: *Great, but we are over our 20 words. What can we do?*

As the students and teacher worked together they edited the summary to the following 20 words:

> "Jackie Robinson was the first black athlete to play baseball. There are many things planned to celebrate the 50th anniversary."

The students then read the next several paragraphs and edited the first summary. As they worked, they evaluated the importance of ideas and kept referring back to the idea of how a news announcer would say this. Then they read on until the end of the article and did the summary one more time.

Follow-up Activities

Once students have reviewed and discussed the information in the reading material, it's usually a good idea to reinforce and extend learning by having them complete one or more related activities. Here are some follow-up activities that would be appropriate for this lesson:

✳ Have students present a news show at the end of a week, using "news flashes" from several pieces they have read.

✳ Encourage students to search the Internet or newspapers for the major news of the day and then create news flashes for a major news story. Students can use the reproducible of page 54 for this activity.

News Flash!

A Major League Hero

By Nick Friedman

Before a man named Jackie Robinson came along, African-Americans were not allowed to play major league baseball. Fifty years ago this spring, Robinson went to bat for the Brooklyn Dodgers, and opened the door for black athletes to play in all pro sports.

To celebrate the 50th anniversary of Robinson's debut, the major leagues have some major plans. This season, players will wear a special patch on their uniform that shows Robinson's signature. The Baseball Hall of Fame in Cooperstown, New York, will feature a new exhibit about Robinson's life. And a souvenir coin with a picture of Robinson will be sold at stadiums around the country.

No Blacks Allowed

In 1947, many people discriminat-ed against blacks because of the color of their skin. In Southern states, for example, segregation laws said blacks could not go to the same schools as whites, swim in the same pools, or even drink from the same water fountains. Baseball-team owners also believed in the segregation of blacks and whites.

Robinson Steps Up

In 1945, Robinson was playing in the Negro Leagues, a baseball league for blacks only. Like many Negro

Easy Strategies and Mini-Lessons That Build Content Area Reading Skills Scholastic Professional Books, 1999

League stars, Robinson had the talent to play in the majors. He could hit with power, run the bases in a flash, and field ground balls with flawless grace.

That same year, one major league owner, Branch Rickey of the Brooklyn Dodgers, decided it was time for a change. He began to scout the Negro Leagues for a star who could crack baseball's color barrier. After much searching, he chose Robinson.

Why Robinson? Because the 26-year-old star was mature, intelligent, and had the will to succeed. He also had the courage and self-control not to respond to racist remarks by getting into fist fights.

Robinson played his first game with the Dodgers on April 15, 1947, wearing the number 42. All that season, he endured racism wherever the Dodgers played. Fans cursed and spit at him. Others threatened to kill him. Opponents tried to knock him down on purpose.

Through all the hardship, Robinson played brilliantly. At the end of the season, he was honored as Rookie of the Year. By the time his 10-year playing career was over, Robinson's talent and courage had changed the opinions many people held about blacks.

In 1962, Robinson became the first black player to be inducted into the Baseball Hall of Fame. He died in 1972, at age 53.

The Negro Leagues

Some of the greatest baseball players in history never got up to bat in the major leagues. They starred in the Negro Leagues.

The Negro Leagues began in 1920. Teams such as the Kansas City Monarchs, Pittsburgh Craw-fords, and Baltimore Black Sox dazzled fans with sparkling play.

But the players had hard lives. They didn't make much money. To earn more, they sometimes played three games a day. Often, players had to sleep on their team bus when racist hotel owners refused to let them stay overnight.

The Negro Leagues ended in 1960. Later, the talent of these great stars was recognized by the major leagues. In 1971, Satchel Paige became the first of 13 Negro League players to be inducted into the Baseball Hall of Fame.

"A Major League Hero" originally appeared in Scholastic News, *February 7, 1997.*

Easy Strategies and Mini-Lessons That Build Content Area Reading Skills Scholastic Professional Books, 1999

Possible Sentences

Strategy Summary

This prereading strategy can be used with both narrative and expository text. Students are given several words from the selection and asked to write one or more sentences that they think they will read in the chapter, article or story. Then they read to find out whether the author has used the words the same way that they did. This strategy is used to activate prior knowledge before reading and to enhance comprehension. When using this strategy, students read with interest and purpose and are actively involved before, during, and after reading.

Before Reading

- Select words from the article that students will be reading. Start with five or six words, then increase the number once students are familiar with the strategy and are ready for a greater challenge. These words should be ones that students can combine in several different ways to make one or more sentences.

- After introducing the words, explain that the purpose of this activity is to make a sentence or sentences using the words in the same way the author has.

● Working in pairs, students discuss the words and speculate about how they are related. Then students write their possible sentences. Encourage them to try to use different combinations of words in several sentences.

● Have students share their sentences with the rest of the class and give reasons for the way they used words. Then have them predict the content of the piece they are about to read.

After the discussion, have students read to find the words. Encourage them to compare their sentences to the author's and to see whether their predictions were accurate.

After Reading

● Have students compare their sentences to the author's. Did they use the words in the same way as the author? Were they accurate in their predictions?

● Discuss the words. Which words were used differently from the way predicted? Which words had a meaning other than one they were familiar with? Which words were the most helpful in figuring out the topic?

● Have students write a summary of the article, highlighting the words they used for this activity.

● As an application, have students create their own mini-word walls using poster board. They can skim the chapter for words that are important to the theme or the topic and put them on their posters. They may illustrate the words if they choose to do so.

In this strategy, the discussion about the connections and relationship between the words is very important. Speculating on the words and how they relate to one another helps build background knowledge and enhances comprehension.

The Strategy in Action

Topic: The Presidency

Text: "What Makes a Great President?" (pages 62 to 65)

Other material: Copies of Possible Sentences (page 61)

To begin the lesson, the teacher put the following words on the board. Then she said, "Today we will be reading the article that I

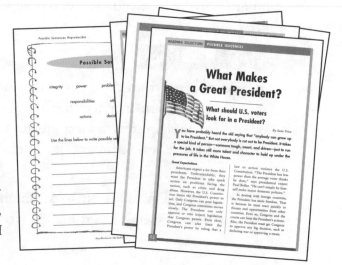

chose these words from. I want you to think about possible sentences that the author may have written using these words. Working in pairs, think about how you could use these words to make sentences that you think you will be reading. Also, discuss what you think the article is about."

integrity   power   problems   character traits

responsibilities   attitude   voters

actions   decide   veto

Students got into pairs and quickly started speculating about how the words could be used to create sentences and trying out different combinations. As the teacher circulated around the room, she listened to the discussions and commented positively on the sentences that groups had constructed. After each pair had at least one sentence, the teacher asked several to share their sentences and also their predictions about the article. Here is a part of that discussion.

Teacher: *You have all had a chance to talk about the words and put them into sentences. Who would like to share a sentence?*

Pair 1: We wrote sentences that tell what good voters do. You know, because the election is next week and we keep seeing these ads on TV about who you should vote for. Anyway, one of our sentences was: "Voters have lots of power when they decide who to vote for."

Pair 2: Yeah, we thought it was about the election too, but we thought maybe it's about who you should vote for. We wrote: "You should vote for someone who has good character traits and lots of integrity."

Pair 3: We used all the words to make one big sentence! Our sentence is: Voters have the power to decide who to vote for based on someone's character traits like integrity, experiences, actions, attitude, and how he solves problems and handles all of his responsibilities.

Pair 4: You didn't use all the words! You left out the word "veto." That was the hardest one for us.

Pair 3: Oh right, we kept trying to figure out how it fit and then I guess we forgot it.

Teacher:	(to Pair 4) *So how did you use the word veto?*
Pair 4:	Well, we said this: "The President sometimes causes problems when he has to veto a law."
Pair 3:	That's why we were having a problem. We didn't think about the President. We were just thinking about another kind of candidate like a city councilman.
Teacher:	*Did the word "veto" make anyone else think of the President?*
Pair 5:	We kept thinking that it was about the election and so we wrote sentences about the President. One sentence we wrote was: "A candidate for president should have good character traits and be ready to handle a lot of power, like when he has to veto a law."
Teacher:	*Good, any more ideas?*

The discussion continued until most of the pairs had a chance to share some of their sentences and speculate about the contents of the article. The teacher did not confirm the topic of the article but kept asking questions about students' reasoning and how they thought the various words were connected. When the discussion was completed, students turned to the article, eagerly searching it to see if any of the sentences they wrote were in the article.

Follow-up Activities

After students have reviewed and discussed the information in the reading material, it's usually a good idea to reinforce and extend learning by having them complete one or more related activities. Here are some follow-up activities that would be appropriate for this lesson:

✳ Challenge students to brainstorm a list of qualities that they think a good president should have. They can turn this list into a voter's guide for selecting a president.

✳ Ask students to search the Internet to find information about previous presidents. Have them use the information to create a chart comparing Presidents. Possible categories for comparison include: age, occupation, birthplace, and major issues faced while in office.

✳ Invite students to search print periodicals or Internet locations to research how other countries elect officials.

✳ Have students conduct a survey asking people how they decide on a candidate to vote for.

Possible Sentences

integrity   power   problems   character traits

responsibilities   attitude   voters

actions   decide   veto

Use the lines below to write possible sentences.

_____

_____

_____

_____

_____

_____

_____

What Makes a Great President?

What should U.S. voters look for in a President?

By Sean Price

Y ou have probably heard the old saying that "anybody can grow up to be President." But not everybody is cut out to be President. It takes a special kind of person—someone tough, smart, and driven—just to run for the job. It takes still more talent and character to hold up under the pressures of life in the White House.

Great Expectations

Americans expect a lot from their presidents. Understandably, they want the President to take quick action on problems facing the nation, such as crime and drug abuse. However, the U.S. Constitution limits the President's power to act. Only Congress can pass legislation, and Congress sometimes moves slowly. The President can only approve or veto (reject) legislation that Congress passes. Even then, Congress can also limit the President's power by ruling that a law or action violates the U.S. Constitution. "The President has less power than the average voter thinks he does," says presidential expert Paul Boller. "He can't simply by himself make major domestic policies."

In dealing with foreign countries, the President has more freedom. That is because he must react quickly to threats and opportunities from other countries. Even so, Congress and the courts can limit the President's actions. Also, the President must get Congress to approve any big decision, such as declaring war or approving a treaty.

Easy Strategies and Mini-Lessons That Build Content Area Reading Skills   Scholastic Professional Books, 1999

The "Bully Pulpit"

Despite these limitations, the President has incredible power. Much of that power is informal, meaning it is not spelled out anywhere in the U.S. Constitution or laws. For instance, President Theodore Roosevelt (in office 1901-1909) said that his office gave him a "bully pulpit"— a powerful platform—that let him draw attention to key issues.

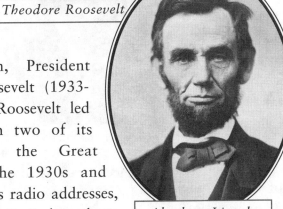
Theodore Roosevelt

Theodore Roosevelt was an expert at using the bully pulpit to drum up support for his policies. So was his cousin, President Franklin D. Roosevelt (1933-1945). Franklin Roosevelt led the U.S. through two of its greatest crises: the Great Depression of the 1930s and World War II. His radio addresses, called "fireside chats," drew huge audiences. Before one speech, Roosevelt asked people to buy maps so that they could follow his explanation of World War II events. His request produced a nationwide run on maps, and about 80 percent of Americans listened to his speech.

Abraham Lincoln

Facing Crises

Franklin Roosevelt is considered one of the best presidents, in part because he was so good at communicating with the public. What other skills do you think the President needs? Consider these three crises faced by past presidents:

- *The Louisiana Purchase:* In 1803, our third president, Thomas Jefferson (1801-1809), had an opportunity that came wrapped in a big problem. France had offered to sell the U.S. a huge chunk of land west of the Mississippi River for just $15 million. That was a bargain. The problem was that the U.S. Constitution gave Jefferson no authority to make the purchase. But Jefferson went ahead and bought the land, nearly doubling the size of the U.S. He later admitted that he had "stretched the Constitution until it cracked." Congress later approved the purchase.

- *Risk of Civil War:* Abraham Lincoln was elected President in November 1860, but he did not take office until the following March. During that time, seven Southern states decided to secede (leave) the Union because they feared that Lincoln would abolish slavery. The new President had to choose: Should he oppose secession and risk civil war, or should he let the Southern states secede and see the U.S. break apart? Lincoln chose to oppose secession. The U.S. Civil War began one month after he became President.

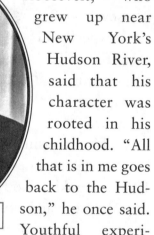

Franklin Roosevelt

• *The Berlin Airlift:* After World War II ended in 1945, the German capital city of Berlin was divided. West Berlin was occupied by troops from the U.S. and its allies; East Berlin was occupied by troops from the Soviet Union. The whole city was located in Soviet controlled East Germany. In June 1948, the Soviets cut off all land routes to West Berlin, trying to force the Western powers out of the city. U.S. President Harry S. Truman (1945-1953) could either back down and lose the respect of his allies, or stand firm and risk starting a war with the Soviets. Instead, he chose to go around the blockade by sending supplies by air. Within a year, the Soviets ended the blockade.

Who Is Best Qualified?

How can voters be sure that a candidate will hold up during those kinds of pressure situations? The short answer is that they can't. Even so, a candidate's character often gives clues as to how the person will react under stress. People disagree about what character traits are most important in a president. But there are some commonly accepted things that people look for, such as integrity, strength, and caring.

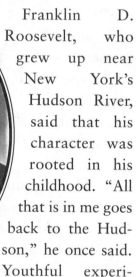

John F. Kennedy

Franklin D. Roosevelt, who grew up near New York's Hudson River, said that his character was rooted in his childhood. "All that is in me goes back to the Hudson," he once said. Youthful experiences are also credited with shaping Bill Clinton and his opponent in the 1996 election, Bob Dole. Experts say that the misfortune that both faced at a young age helped make them very determined men.

For instance, 14-year-old Bill Clinton was a star student in Hot Springs, Arkansas. He seemed to

Easy Strategies and Mini-Lessons That Build Content Area Reading Skills Scholastic Professional Books, 1999

excel at everything he did. Yet his sunny attitude and good grades masked terrible problems at home. His stepfather was an alcoholic who abused Clinton's mother. Clinton testified at their divorce trial that he had tried to stop his stepfather's violence. In response, he said, the older man "threatened to mash my face in."

On the other hand, Bob Dole was a shy, athletic boy who grew up during the Great Depression in a poor neighborhood of Russell, Kansas. At 19, he joined the U.S. Army to fight in World War II. When he was 21, Dole was wounded twice. His wounds almost killed him and they left his right arm useless. "I do try harder," Dole once said. "If I didn't, I'd be sitting in a rest home, in a rocker, drawing disability [pay]."

Washington's Struggle

Experts say that adult experiences can be just as important in shaping a future president. "It's their adult experiences that help them form their [political] opinions," says presidential expert Joan Hoff. For instance, during the American Revolution, General George Washington struggled to keep the Continental Army going. He received

Bill Clinton

little help from the 13 states, and the Continental Congress had no power to force the states to pitch in. As a result of that experience, Washington pushed hard while he was President (1789-1797) to create a strong central U.S. government.

Paul Boller says that it sometimes is difficult to compare modern candidates with the candidates of the past. In the first place, technological advances such as television allow the press to follow every move that a modern candidate makes. Second, Boller says, people's attitudes about both Presidents and candidates often become more romantic with the passage of time. "George Washington is rightly considered a model character," Boller says. "[But when he was President,] he had enemies who didn't think he had any [good qualities] at all."

Passing the Test

How important is character in deciding which candidate to vote for? Some experts say that voters today worry more about the issues: what the candidates plan to do about crime, health care, education, and other problems. What do you look for in a President?

"What Makes A Great President" originally appeared in Scholastic News, *September 6, 1996.*

Read • Talk • Write

Strategy Summary

As students read informational text, they pause periodically, close the book, and restate what they have learned from the text to a partner, then write down what they learned. This strategy helps students read more attentively, monitor their comprehension, and explain the ideas in their own words. Once they learn how do this with a partner, they can do it when they are studying independently. The basic steps are:

READ, then close the book.

TALK to a partner about what you read.

WRITE what you learned.

Introducing the Strategy

In planning the lesson, choose a short selection of text for students to read, such as part of a textbook chapter or an article. Also decide how to divide the text into four or five shorter segments. Most of the students should be able to read one of these segments in about five minutes.

Tell students you are going to show them a strategy that will help them improve their comprehension and that they will be working with partners to learn it. Then, using the first paragraph or two of the text, model the steps as follows:

1. Read the text silently while students read along silently.

2. Close the book and tell the class what you remember reading. If you like, invite them to add any points you might have forgotten.

3. On the board or an overhead transparency, write what you expressed orally. Use your own words and call students' attention to this, stressing that the point of your talking and writing is to test your own understanding of the material, not to parrot the author's exact language.

4. Scan the original text to see if there is any important information you haven't already covered. Invite students to do this along with you. Add any important points to your written notes and correct any factual errors.

Guiding the Practice

Tell students they will read the rest of the selection in segments, each time stopping to talk with their partner, write, and reread to check their accuracy. Make sure each student has paper and a pencil ready.

- Have students organize themselves into pairs, with one person designated as "A" and the other "B." If there's an odd number in the class, you may want to pair up with a student rather than have a group of three. Explain the roles of talker and listener: The talker engages in sustained talking while the listener just listens. The listener does not correct the talker or comment on how the talker is doing.

- Assign the next segment of text to be read and have students mark the end point with a paper clip or other marker. Tell students they should begin reading silently when you say "start" and should not read beyond the marker. Remind them to read with concentration so that they will be able to look away from the text and tell their partner what they learned in the way you just modeled. When everyone is ready, give the signal to start.

- Call "time" at the end of four or five minutes, even if some students have not finished. (A student doesn't need to have read the whole segment to be able to do the next steps.) Have students close the book or cover the text so they will not look at it when they talk.

- Announce which one of the pairs, A or B, is to talk first. Have all the talkers start talking at once (each to his or her partner) when you give the signal. Let them talk for a minute or two. Talking time can be extended as students become more familiar with the activity and are improving their performance.

- When time is up, have those who listened take their turn at talking. Tell them they can say the same things their partners just said if they want to but that they should restate the ideas in their own words and should try to add new information if they can.

- When the second talkers have finished, have everyone write individually for two or three minutes, or perhaps longer if they are writing intently, to express what they learned about the topic.

- Finally, have partners look back at the text briefly to check facts, correct errors, and clarify points, adding to or revising their notes as needed.

- Repeat the steps for each of the other segments of text. With each new round, you may want to change the designated first talker. But be sure to wait until students have finished reading before you announce who talks first so that everyone will be encouraged to concentrate and read carefully.

Reflecting on the Strategy

When the group has finished reading the full text, have them discuss their reactions to the strategy. The following questions can be used to prompt reflection and self-evaluation:

- What did you find most difficult about this?

- What was relatively easy?

- Is it better to be the first talker or the second talker? Why?

- Did the talking and writing help you understand and remember the material? Why?

- Did the reading and concentrating get easier or harder with each new segment of text?

- As you were reading, what did you do to help your concentration so you could really pay attention to what the words said?

- How could you improve your ability to use this strategy?

- When might you use this strategy on your own?

Offer your own comments, too, if you like. For instance, you might say something like this: It can seem a lot harder to put the text aside and state what you read than to simply read to begin with. That's because when we think we're reading just fine, we may not be concentrating very well. Most people also think talking and writing help them understand and remember what they read because they're really thinking about what the words say rather than just pronouncing the words to themselves. A text usually seems easier as you work through it with this strategy, probably because what you read first helps you to understand what comes later. This is a good strategy to use when you're studying on your own, because it can help you understand the material better. It's also good to use when you're working on a report. Talking first helps you use your own words when you write instead of copying from the book.

The Strategy in Action

Topic: Endangered Species

Text: "Whose Home Is It, Anyway?"
(pages 73 to 74)

Other material: Overhead transparency or individual copies of Read•Talk•Write (page 72)

At the start of the lesson, the teacher modeled the strategy by reading the first two paragraphs of the article silently as students followed on their own copies. Then the teacher looked up and turned the paper over, asking the students to do the same. In modeling the talking step, the teacher spoke conversationally to avoid sounding like a formal report.

Teacher: *First, I learned that this article is about endangered species. Those are animals that are in danger of dying out altogether, which is what "becoming extinct" means. The article starts out by saying that probably most people think it's great to save animals from dying out, but there are some people who are not so sure about this. They think when too much effort goes into saving an animal species from extinction, it could end up hurting people. For instance, if people have to stop harvesting trees or using the land in other ways to protect an endangered animal, they might lose their jobs, and that would be really serious. So people have really different opinions about this. I think that's about it. Does anyone have anything to add? Don't look back at the text yet! Just see if you can remember anything that I didn't talk about.*

Student 1: It said something about the government in there, but I don't remember just what.

69

Teacher: *Good point. I remember that now. It said that the government is often the one running the programs to protect endangered animals. Anyone else? No? Okay, then let's see if I can write this all down.*

The teacher wrote the following on an overhead transparency while the students watched.

Many people think it's important to save animals that are close to becoming extinct, and the government is involved in many save-the-animal programs. But there are some people who don't agree. They say it's not right to save an animal when it means a lot of people have to lose their jobs or have their lives messed up. Some of the people who are not real positive about saving endangered animals are people like farmers or loggers, who live off the land. There are real differences of opinion between those people and the ones who want to save endangered animals.

Teacher: *Now I want to look at the text again to see if there's anything I missed. You all can look too. Does anyone see anything I didn't put in writing?*

Student 2: There's that part about the tug-of-war. You didn't put that in. I don't get that, though. What does that mean?

Teacher: *You're right that I didn't use those words. I wanted to say the same idea in my own words, so I wrote this (pointing to the last sentence). Saying that two sides are in a tug-of-war means that each side feels strongly about an issue and each side tries to "pull" the others over to their side, to make them believe the way they believe.*

Next, the teacher had the class organize into pairs and had them decide who would be A and who would be B. He had decided to have the class read the section entitled "The Case of the Condor" first, and then "Government Gets in on the Act." Circulating as the students talked after the first reading time, he heard statements like these:

Student 1: It said that some people were trying to save condors and they had some little ones and they were going to put them in cages outside. I guess those people were government people. Some other people were upset about it, and they said the government shouldn't tell them what to do.

Student 2: The people thought the condor thing would be like another time before, when they weren't allowed to cut down trees and stuff. Some animal was in the forest. I don't remember what it was, but the government was trying to save it so they wouldn't let anyone cut down the trees and the people got upset because it meant they lost a lot of business.

When pairs were finished talking, students wrote as much as they could remember, still not looking back at the text. Here are two samples of their writing:

> Condors are in danger. People who were trying to save them had some baby birds they wanted to put outside in big cages. Other people didn't want the birds there. They were afraid they might not be able to do their work if the condors were there because they would have to be watching out for the condors all the time.

> Some people didn't like what the government was doing to save condors. They thought they would lose their jobs because they would have to be real careful around the birds they put outside. Like if they had a job cutting down trees maybe they wouldn't be able to cut down trees because the condors were there.

Follow-up Activities

After students have used read•talk•write strategy under supervision enough times so that they are familiar with it, use it regularly in these ways:

✳ Have students apply read•talk•write to reading assignments they complete outside of class. Encourage students to share how they use the strategy in class discussions and give each other tips on how they maintain concentration, read to remember, and sustain their talking and writing about the topic.

✳ In science or social studies, first introduce the selection with a good pre-reading strategy such as an anticipation guide or the key word strategy. Have students read once to satisfy their first purposes. Then have them reread, using read•talk•write to focus on more difficult sections, clarify information, and reinforce learning.

✳ When students are looking up information for reports, have them pair up and use the read•talk•write strategy with their source material. It's all right for each member of the pair to be reading different material if students are familiar with the strategy.

✳ When students are used to the strategy, add a twist to the rereading step. After students have written, have them raise questions they would like to answer by looking back at the text. For instance, they might want to check a date or a name, or look for the third fact if they could only remember two. Have them state their rereading purpose orally and then reread.

71

Read

Read the text silently with good concentration.
Then close the book.

Talk

Talk to your partner about what you read.
State the ideas in your own words.
Then listen to your partner talk.

Write

Write what you learned. Use your own words.
Try not to use the exact words of the text.

Easy Strategies and Mini-Lessons That Build Content Area Reading Skills Scholastic Professional Books, 1999

Ranchers near Yellowstone National Park are learning to live with a new neighbor—the endangered gray wolf. But can all Americans learn to live with the government's endangered species program?

Whose Home Is It, Anyway?

By Mi Won Kim

Does your heart soar when an animal flies back from the brink of extinction? Every one would cheer the return of an endangered species, right? Wrong. Some people say that the government's efforts to save endangered animals put people in danger.

Many farmers, loggers, and landowners say that they must give up their right to cut trees and use land where endangered species live. This has caused a tug-of-war between people who want to protect wildlife and people who want to protect their jobs and livelihoods.

The Case of the Condor

Earlier this year, the endangered California condor was trapped in the center of this clash. Months of debate finally set it free. In the next few weeks, scientists are planning to place six young condors in huge outdoor cages in Arizona. But residents in Arizona and nearby Utah nearly grounded the government's plan to bring this bird back.

For local officials in Utah, the California condor brought back bad memories. They had felt threatened by other attempts to save animals under the Endangered Species Act. This law forbids people from harming endangered species or the land where they live. "Government officials shouldn't tell us what to do with

Easy Strategies and Mini-Lessons That Build Content Area Reading Skills Scholastic Professional Books, 1999

Stamp Out Extinction

How does a plant or animal get on the endangered-species list? Here's how:

- A scientist, lawmaker, or any American citizen suggests a plant or animal as a candidate for the endangered-species list. The person writes to the FWS and explains why the species needs the government's help and protection.

- The FWS asks scientists and other experts to check out the plant or animal. These experts ask themselves if the species is:
  - sick or in danger
  - living in an unhealthy environment
  - not protected by any laws at all

- If the answer to any of those questions is yes, the FWS holds public hearings. Lawyers, scientists, and anyone else can speak at these hearings. If there is enough scientific proof that protection is needed, wildlife experts propose the species for listing. Once the director of the FWS approves the decision, the species is put on the endangered-species list.

our land," Maloy Dodds told *Scholastic News*. Dodds is the commissioner of Garfield County in Utah. "For years, sawmills in our area were closing down because we weren't allowed to cut trees in forests where peregrine falcons lived."

Scientist Robert Mesta was shocked when residents protested the government's condor recovery plan. He works for the U.S. Fish and Wildlife Service (FWS), the main government agency in charge of enforcing the Endangered Species Act. "The condor isn't a threat to people or their land. But people are nervous about their jobs and futures, so they blame their problems on endangered species," he told *SN*.

Government wildlife experts and residents finally reached an agreement. Scientists will set the condors free, and landowners can continue living as they always have—as long as they don't try to hurt the condor on purpose.

Government Gets In On the Act

Some members of the federal government have not made peace with the endangered-species program. In March of 1995, Congress members shut down the FWS's power to list new endangered species. This shutdown lasted for 13 months. Congress also voted to give less money to the FWS in 1996 than in 1995. This means that the service has less money to buy land and design programs to save endangered species.

Now government wildlife experts have a big job to do with less money. More than 400 animals and plants are waiting for possible placement on the endangered-species list.

Robert Mesta hopes that the California condor will soar as an example of how the government and landowners can successfully work together to save species. He believes the condor project will rebuild the condor population—and trust between citizens and the federal government. "Communities that were once violently opposed to us now support our goals," he told *Scholastic News*.

"Whose Home Is It, Anyway? originally appeared in Scholastic News, *September 27, 1996.*

Easy Strategies and Mini-Lessons That Build Content Area Reading Skills Scholastic Professional Books, 1999

Strip Story

Strategy Summary

Using either expository or narrative material, students rearrange sentences or paragraphs that have been mixed up. They discuss the order that they think makes sense, then put the sentences or paragraphs in that order. The key to this strategy is making sure that students focus not on finding the correct order but on the rationale they use to determine that order. This strategy helps build comprehension by giving students an opportunity to understand how a text is constructed and how the parts relate to one another. Students' writing abilities will also be strengthened as they are given opportunities to think and reason as writers.

Before Reading

- Select a short story or an article for students to work with. You may want to start with sentences within a paragraph and then, once students are comfortable with the strategy, move them to longer pieces and have them rearrange by paragraphs. Be aware that sometimes ordering paragraphs may be easier than ordering a short set of sentences with a complex pattern.

- Prepare the material by putting the sentences (or paragraphs) from a text in a mixed-up order and making copies for students to work with.

- Present the prepared passage to the students and have them read the piece silently. Then ask, "Does this text make sense to you? Why not?" Explain that their job will be to rearrange the elements so that the piece as a whole makes sense.

- Have students brainstorm about the clues that might be helpful when they rearrange the elements. Point out the role of transition words and pronouns that refer to nouns and explain that both are helpful in determining order.

- Allow students to work in pairs or small groups, depending on the length of the material to be read. When two or more students work on the reordering together, they help each other's thinking. First they should cut the sentences (or paragraphs) apart so that they can move the elements around on their desktops as they decide how best to reorder them.

- As students are working, encourage them to move the sentences and paragraphs several times until they find an arrangement that makes sense. As you walk around, listen for the clues that they are using to determine order, intervening if necessary with suggestions.

After Reading

- Have each pair of students get together with another pair to compare their arrangements. Encourage them to explain their rationale and the textual clues they used. Point out that their arrangements do not have to be exactly alike as long as they make sense.

- Make a list of the transition words or phrases students found as they were working. Also keep a list of reasons students had for placing items in a particular order. For example, "We put this paragraph first because it explained what the whole article was about." Keep this list posted as a resource for this activity throughout the year.

- Have students apply what they have learned by using transition words and phrases in their writing. Or, as a center activity, have them find and prepare articles or stories for others to rearrange.

When students are working on a strip story, the reasoning behind the way they order the sentences or paragraphs should be the focus. Students should be able to articulate why they chose to arrange the elements in a specific order. This will help them notice the organizational devices and signals in various texts and begin using them in their own writing.

The Strategy in Action

Topic: Immigration

Text: "The Newest Americans"
(pages 83 to 84)

Other materials: Strip Story reproducible
(pages 81 to 82)

At the beginning of the lesson, the teacher put the following paragraphs on the overhead and, as she handed out a copy to each student, said, "Today we will be working on an article that is very interesting but right now doesn't make sense. Take a look at this and tell me what you think is wrong."

The Newest Americans

Like René, thousands of people immigrate to America every day to start new lives. Last year, about 720,000 of these newcomers entered the U.S. legally. About 300,000 other immigrants entered without permission from the U.S. They are considered illegal.

René Gutierrez has big dreams for the future. He wants to teach karate. He wants to have a large family. And, he wants to become a United States citizen.

Why the big wave? Most immigrants flee from their native countries because of war, oppression, or poverty. Later they are joined by their families. René's father moved here from Mexico in 1993 because he could not find a job. René joined him in 1994. Today, René's father, who was a veterinarian in Mexico, works in a bagel store in René's new hometown, Brooklyn, New York.

René was born in Mexico. He came to America three years ago as part of a tidal wave of immigration that has been surging since 1990.

The Immigration Debate

Despite the backlash against the recent immigration wave, some Americans say immigrants make our country strong. They bring with them fresh ideas and a drive to succeed.

Congress has passed two new laws in response to these concerns. One law makes it harder for immigrants living here to bring family members over. The other law limits the amount of government benefits immigrants can receive.

René will have to wait until he is 18 to apply to become a citizen. That's the law.

But if his father becomes a citizen before then, René automatically becomes one too.

Either way, one thing is clear: Immigrants have always been a part of our nation's history. From the Pilgrims, who came from England and landed on Plymouth Rock, to Mexican kids like René, people from all over come here to take a shot at the American Dream.

The American Dream is the idea that you can come here with very little, work hard, and make a better life. For most immigrants, the dream is not complete until they do one thing: become a U.S. citizen. Citizens are entitled to the benefits all Americans receive.

Whenever the U.S. experiences a big wave of immigration, some Americans worry. They say immigrants take jobs away from people who were born here. They also argue that immigrants cost our nation money because they sometimes receive government benefits.

Becoming a Citizen

René can't wait to be a citizen. Meanwhile, he will keep doing the things other kids do. He'll play video games, draw comic-book figures, and hang out. "I love being in America!," says René.

To apply for citizenship, René's father must prove that he has lived in the U.S. legally for at least five years. He has to show that he has obeyed the law and that he can read, write, speak, and understand basic English. He will also take a test on U.S. history and government.

After students pointed out that the paragraphs were out of order, the teacher had them cut the story into paragraphs and, working in pairs, reorder the paragraphs. This is part of the discussion that followed the activity:

Teacher:	*What words or phrases helped you figure out how to reorder the paragraphs?*
Student 1:	In the first part we read the paragraph that said there was a tidal wave of immigrants. Then we found the paragraph that started with "Why the big wave?" so we figured it was talking about the tidal wave in the other paragraph, so it should follow that paragraph.
Student 2:	Yes, we used that same clue. At first we thought it was easy to figure out which paragraph went first because all the way through the article it kept mentioning René, so we thought that it should start with all the information about René.
Student 3:	Except that when we started, we put the paragraph that says he

was born in Mexico first.

Teacher: *So why did you change it?*

Student 3: Well, when we read it again we found the words about the tidal wave, and then we realized that the next paragraph had to start with "Why the big wave?"

Teacher: *What other clues were helpful?*

Student 4: In the second section, the author mentioned the American Dream. And then there was the paragraph that explained what the American Dream was, so we knew it had to follow that paragraph.

Teacher: *Were there any parts that were especially hard to figure out?*

Student 5: We kept moving the paragraph about the backlash against recent immigrants around. It seemed like it could go anywhere in that second section.

Teacher: *So where did you finally place it?*

Student 5: Well, we put it first in the second section, but I'm still not sure it goes first.

Teacher: *Why not?*

Student 5: Well, it just doesn't sound right.

Teacher: *Did anyone else have a problem with that paragraph?*

Student 6: We did. But we ended up putting it after the paragraph about the laws that Congress has passed. We knew that the Congress paragraph had to follow the paragraph about government benefits, so it was the only logical place for it.

The discussion continued along these lines. As students were giving their reasons, the teacher was listing clue words and phrases on the board. Several groups differed on the order of the paragraphs, and one group persuaded another group to change their order. The students read and reread the article many times to figure out the order, which resulted in deeper understanding of the information in the article and active consideration of principles of text organization. To wrap-up this activity, the teacher handed out the original article for students to read.

Follow-up Activities

After students have reviewed and discussed the information in the reading material, it's usually a good idea to reinforce and extend learning by having students complete one or more related activities. Here are some follow-up activities that would be appropriate for this lesson:

✳ Once students are familiar with the strip story strategy, have them try using the strategy with both a narrative and an expository text. Present students with a narrative text that has been reordered and an expository text that has been reordered. Challenge students to work on putting both texts in order. Then, have students compare the clues that they used for each type of writing. Have them reflect on which type of passage was easier to reorganize and why.

✳ Have students make a list of the words and phrases that help them figure out the order of a piece of text. Then have them try writing a short piece that uses the words and phrases that they have encountered.

✳ Challenge students to create their own strip story packets to give to other students. Students can find appropriate stories or articles and rearrange the order. Place the stories in a learning center for students to work on independently or in small groups.

VERSION #1

The Newest Americans

Like René, thousands of people immigrate to America every day to start new lives. Last year, about 720,000 of these newcomers entered the U.S. legally. About 300,000 other immigrants entered without permission from the U.S. They are considered illegal.

René Gutierrez has big dreams for the future. He wants to teach karate. He wants to have a large family. And, he wants to become a United States citizen.

Why the big wave? Most immigrants flee from their native countries because of war, oppression, or poverty. Later they are joined by their families. René's father moved here from Mexico in 1993 because he could not find a job. René joined him in 1994. Today, René's father, who was a veterinarian in Mexico, works in a bagel store in René's new hometown, Brooklyn, New York.

René was born in Mexico. He came to America three years ago as part of a tidal wave of immigration that has been surging since 1990.

The Immigration Debate

Despite the backlash against the recent immigration wave, some Americans say immigrants make our country strong. They bring with them fresh ideas and a drive to succeed.

Easy Strategies and Mini-Lessons That Build Content Area Reading Skills Scholastic Professional Books, 1999

Congress has passed two new laws in response to these concerns. One law makes it harder for immigrants living here to bring family members over. The other law limits the amount of government benefits immigrants can receive.

René will have to wait until he is 18 to apply to become a citizen. That's the law. But if his father becomes a citizen before then, René automatically becomes one too.

Either way, one thing is clear: Immigrants have always been a part of our nation's history. From the Pilgrims who came from England and landed on Plymouth Rock, to Mexican kids like René, people from all over come here to take a shot at the American Dream.

The American Dream is the idea that you can come here with very little, work hard, and make a better life. For most immigrants, the dream is not complete until they do one thing: become a U.S. citizen. Citizens are entitled to the benefits all Americans receive.

Whenever the U.S. experiences a big wave of immigration, some Americans worry. They say immigrants take jobs away from people who were born here. They also argue that immigrants cost our nation money because they sometimes receive government benefits.

Becoming a Citizen

René can't wait to be a citizen. Meanwhile, he will keep doing the things other kids do. He'll play video games, draw comic-book figures, and hang out. "I love being in America!" says René.

To apply for citizenship, René's father must prove that he has lived in the U.S. legally for at least five years. He has to show that he has obeyed the law, and that he can read, write, speak, and understand basic English. He will also take a test on U.S. history and government.

Easy Strategies and Mini-Lessons That Build Content Area Reading Skills Scholastic Professional Books, 1999

VERSION #2

The Newest Americans

By Nick Friedman

In the first five years of this decade, more immigrants entered the United States than at any other time since the 1920s. What's behind this tidal wave of immigration?

René Gutierrez has big dreams for the future. He wants to teach karate. He wants to have a large family. And, he wants to become a United States citizen.

René was born in Mexico. He came to America three years ago as part of a tidal wave of immigration that has been surging since 1990.

Why the big wave? Most immigrants flee from their native countries because of war, oppression or poverty. Later, they are joined by their families. René's father moved here from Mexico in 1993 because he could not find a job. René joined him in 1994. Today, René's father, who was a veterinarian in Mexico, works in a bagel store in René's new home-town, Brooklyn, New York.

Like René, thousands of people immigrate to America every day to start new lives. Last year, about 720,000 of these newcomers entered the U.S. legally. About 300,000 other immigrants entered without permission from the U.S. They are considered illegal.

The Immigration Debate

Whenever the U.S. experiences a big wave of immigration, some Americans worry. They say immigrants take jobs away from people who were born here. They also argue that immigrants cost our nation money because they sometimes receive government benefits.

Easy Strategies and Mini-Lessons That Build Content Area Reading Skills Scholastic Professional Books, 1999

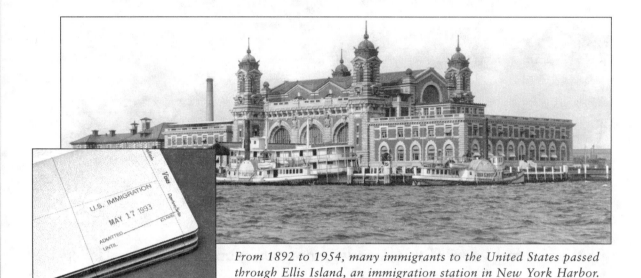

From 1892 to 1954, many immigrants to the United States passed through Ellis Island, an immigration station in New York Harbor.

Congress has passed two new laws in response to these concerns. One law makes it harder for immigrants living here to bring family members over. The other law limits the amount of government benefits immigrants can receive.

Despite the backlash against the recent immigration wave, some Americans say immigrants make our country strong. They bring with them fresh ideas and a drive to succeed.

Either way, one thing is clear: Immigrants have always been a part of our nation's history. From the Pilgrims, who came from England and landed on Plymouth Rock, to Mexican kids like René, people from all over come here to take a shot at the American Dream.

The American Dream is the idea that you can come here with very little, work hard, and make a better life. For most immigrants, the dream is not complete until they do one thing: become a U.S. citizen. Citizens are entitled to the benefits all Americans receive.

René will have to wait until he is 18 to apply to become a citizen. That's the law. But if his father becomes a citizen before then, René automatically becomes one too.

Becoming a Citizen

To apply for citizenship, René's father must prove that he has lived in the U.S. legally for at least five years. He has to show that he has obeyed the law, and that he can read, write, speak, and understand basic English. He will also take a test on U.S. history and government.

René can't wait to be a citizen. Meanwhile, he will keep doing the things other kids do. He'll play video games, draw comic-book figures, and hang out. "I love being in America!," says René.

"The Newest Americans" originally appeared in Scholastic News, *February 21, 1997.*

Easy Strategies and Mini-Lessons That Build Content Area Reading Skills Scholastic Professional Books, 1999

Team Webbing

Strategy Summary

This is an after-reading strategy for reviewing informational text. When students have finished reading and discussing the material, they work in teams to create webs that show what they've learned. Each team creates its own web, then adds to each other team's web in turn. When teams return to their original webs, they review what has been added, raising questions, revising, and elaborating on the information. This strategy engages students in reviewing what they learned and stating it in their own words. It's more motivating than traditional review because it involves interesting ways of interacting with and collaborating with teammates.

Creating a Home Web

First, each team sets up its own web, deciding what information they think is most important to include in it. Here's how to get the teams started.

- Organize students into groups of four to six, each of which has a home station—a table, desks pushed together, or generous floor space. Give team members pencils or markers of a distinctive color. That is, the members of one team might use the color blue while other teams use red, black, green, or other colors. You may want to keep sets of inexpensive colored pencils or markers to use for this activity. Along with writing implements, give each team a piece of sturdy unlined paper that is at least 12 by 18 inches. If sheets this size or larger are not available, tape smaller sheets together to make a good-sized writing area for each team.

● Announce the topic and tell students they will be creating webs of information to show what they have learned about it. Explain that each team starts its home web by writing the topic in a circle in the center of the paper and then deciding on three or four categories of information about that topic it thinks are especially important. Teams should arrange the categories around the center topic, leaving room for other categories to be added and leaving plenty of room for information to be clustered around each category. If students have not done webbing before, show them models like the ones on page 90.

● Go over these rules for making entries on a home web:

1. Each team member must write at least one piece of information but may write more.

2. There must be at least one item in each category.

3. Each team member must add a different piece of information.

4. Students must recall learned information and write it in their own words. Looking at source material is not allowed at this point.

Teams should discuss what they want to include and give thought to planning their webs. For instance, they should discuss a number of ideas and decide which ones the various team members will put on the web. You may require that the information be stated in sentences, or you may allow just words or phrases to be used. Consider allowing sketches, as well. Give students enough time for this first step so that they will end up with a good foundation web.

Visiting Other Webs

After each team has created its web, tell students they will leave their home stations, move to the next station when you give the signal, and add information to that web. Establish a rule for moving, for example, in clockwise order. Here are the rules for visiting a web:

● Teams take their pencils or markers with them and use them for writing on the next web. This way, the team's contributions will be identifiable by color.

● Each team should move to the next web as quickly and quietly as possible with a minimum of horsing around.

- Teams must read everything on the web they are visiting before they decide what new information to add. "New information" means information that is not already on the web. Team members must discuss their ideas because, as before, each student must add at least one new piece of information but may not add the same information as a teammate.

- Additions can be made only to existing categories on a web. New categories may be added only by the team that created the web.

- As before, looking at source material is not allowed, and all information should be in students' own words.

Give the signal to move. Allow a reasonable amount of time for this second step. You may want to circulate to monitor the work, giving reminders and encouragement. Then have teams visit the next web and again read, discuss, and add information. This continues until every team has visited every other web, at which time teams return to their home stations.

Reflecting on Home Webs

Back at their home webs, teams should study the additions that other students have made to their own web. Here are some activities that you might ask students to do at this point as a whole class. Choose one or two to do the same day. Do more over the course of several days.

- Check the additions in each category to make sure they belong. If some additions don't seem to fit the category, students should ask the team that added the information to explain its reasoning.

- Raise questions about the meaning of additions. If any words or ideas are not clear, students should ask the team who added the information to explain what it meant.

- Raise questions about the accuracy of additions. Any team may challenge the accuracy of any information that has been added to its web. Disputes should be settled by checking the original source materials.

- Reread the original materials for any important information that might now be added to the web. Students should, as before, put newly added information in their own words.

- Add more information that students may have picked up from studying other teams' webs. They should be sure that whatever they add is clear and accurate.

- Decide, for each category, which piece of information is the most interesting and why. Each team can present its decision to the whole class.

● Compare and contrast all the teams' webs. A good way to accomplish this is to have the teams line their webs on the board and then discuss as a whole class the similarities and differences in the way their webs are designed and in the categories and information they contain.

The Strategy in Action

Topic: Leonardo da Vinci

Text: "Leonardo da Vinci, Renaissance Man" (pages 93 to 96)

Other materials: Copies of Team Webbing (page 92)

When students were reading and discussing this article, they observed that it contained quite a lot of information about this fascinating man. The teacher, seeing a good opportunity, decided to have them use team webbing to review and reinforce the details they had been discussing. He organized the class into five teams and handed out the materials they needed. He had previously taught students this strategy, and they had practiced it several times, so he was confident they would be able to do a good job. He told them that this time, each group would have to select four categories, no more and no less, and that each person could add only one idea to each web and that it should always be the most interesting piece of information he or she could think of. Also, instead of writing in complete sentences (as they had done before), they could use just words or phrases. As teams worked on their home webs, the teacher circulated to monitor the discussions and offer suggestions. Here are parts of his exchanges with two different groups:

Teacher: (after a few minutes of watching the red-pencil group of five students) *You've got four good categories selected.* (These were: Growing Up, His Art, Inventions, and Interesting Facts.) *Tell me why you decided on them.*

Student 1: Well, the article had stuff about when he was young, so that's why we decided on Growing Up. Then, uh, he's an artist, so we decided that was important to put in.

Student 2: And he invented some neat stuff, too, so we wanted to put that in. And we wanted to put in the stuff about the practical jokes and his handwriting.

Student 3: We all thought that stuff was interesting, so that's why we decided on the last category.

Teacher: *Sounds good. Looks like you're ready to start putting in information. Have you decided what you want to put under Inventions?*

Student 2: Not yet. I think we should put the helicopter in. I think that's really neat that he invented a helicopter. I mean, he lived long ago, before anybody knew about flying, but he did.

Student 3: I want to put in about the bicycle.

Teacher: *You like to go cycling, don't you?*

Student 3: Yes! That's why I think it's neat that he invented the bicycle!

Teacher: *Well, as a team, you'll have to decide what to do.*

Student 4: Maybe we could put both the ideas in. There are five of us and four categories, so we can have two things in one of our categories.

Teacher: *Yes, you could. That's one option if everyone else agrees. Okay, keep up the good work.*

Teacher: (addressing the green-pencil group of six students) *How are you doing?*

Student 6: We can't decide on our last category. (The group had listed three categories on scrap paper: Jobs, Accomplishments, and History of His Life.) We can't think of a fourth one.

Teacher: *What do you mean by "jobs"?*

Student 7: It said how he was a scientist and he designed costumes and he invented things. Those are like jobs, right?

Teacher: *Well, they weren't jobs the way we think of jobs today. Those were just things that he did. Remember, his work was as an artist, a painter.*

Student 8: And then his accomplishments would be like the stuff he invented. Musical instruments and other stuff.

Student 7: But wait. If he didn't really do those things as jobs, then maybe we should put those two categories together. Jobs and Accomplishments. If all that stuff is just stuff he did, then it would all be accomplishments, right?

Student 6: Yeah, I see.

89

Student 8: So then we'd have just two categories, and we need two more!

Teacher: *Well, keep thinking. You're off to a good start.*

In these ways, the teacher provided some guidance but avoided trying to direct the students too much so that they would have to think through what they were doing instead of relying on him to tell them. When all the teams had finished this first step, their webs contained the following categories. Although each set was somewhat different, each reflected important information. Because of the differences, students had to think carefully about what to add to each web as they moved from one to the next.

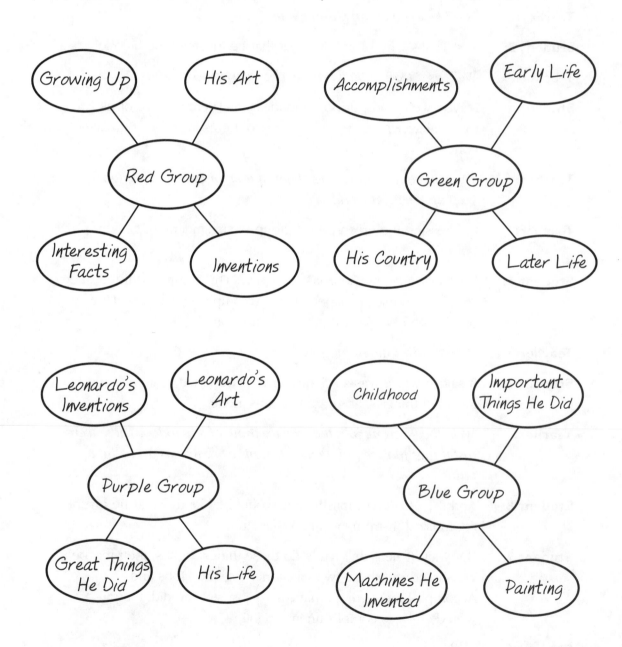

When teams had rotated through all the webs and were back at their home webs, they were very interested in reading what the other groups had added, and there were many questions and comments. Some groups questioned information that they thought had been added to the wrong categories, while others questioned the accuracy of points, having found information in the article to prove their contentions. For instance, one student pointed out that Leonardo didn't invent the bicycle in the 1800s, which some-one put on his home web, because he died in 1519. Another noticed that someone had written, "Sir Pero, Leonardo's father," on her group's web when the name should have been "Ser Piero." Most of the talk, though, focused on how the students had organized their webs. By comparing their webs, for instance, they saw how some of their cate-gories were almost identical, though given different titles.

Follow-up Activities

After students have completed a team webbing session, it's useful to reinforce and extend their learning of both the content and the strategy. Here are suggestions for each type of reinforcement that would be appropriate after this lesson:

* To reinforce content learning: Have students search for more information about Leonardo in books and on the Internet. The focus could be not only to get new information to add to the webs but also to check the accuracy of the information in the article.

* To reinforce content learning: Have students use what they learned in inter-esting ways. For instance, they might make colorful posters with highlights about Leonardo to place in the hall, or they might create a computerized mul-timedia presentation on his life, incorporating special graphics and audio effects along with text.

* To reinforce strategy learning: Have students evaluate how well they did at the team webbing activity. Students could discuss such questions as these: Did everyone read the contents of each web before adding new information? Did team members discuss what each one would add each time? Did team decision making include input from all members? Did the groups move qui-etly and efficiently from web to web?

* To reinforce strategy learning: After evaluating their skill in using the strate-gy, have the class set goals for the next time they do team webbing. Write the goals on a poster and go over them the next time you organize a team webbing activity. Goals might include such things as studying webs more carefully as a visitor before adding information, and discussing information more thoroughly within teams to improve accuracy and clarity.

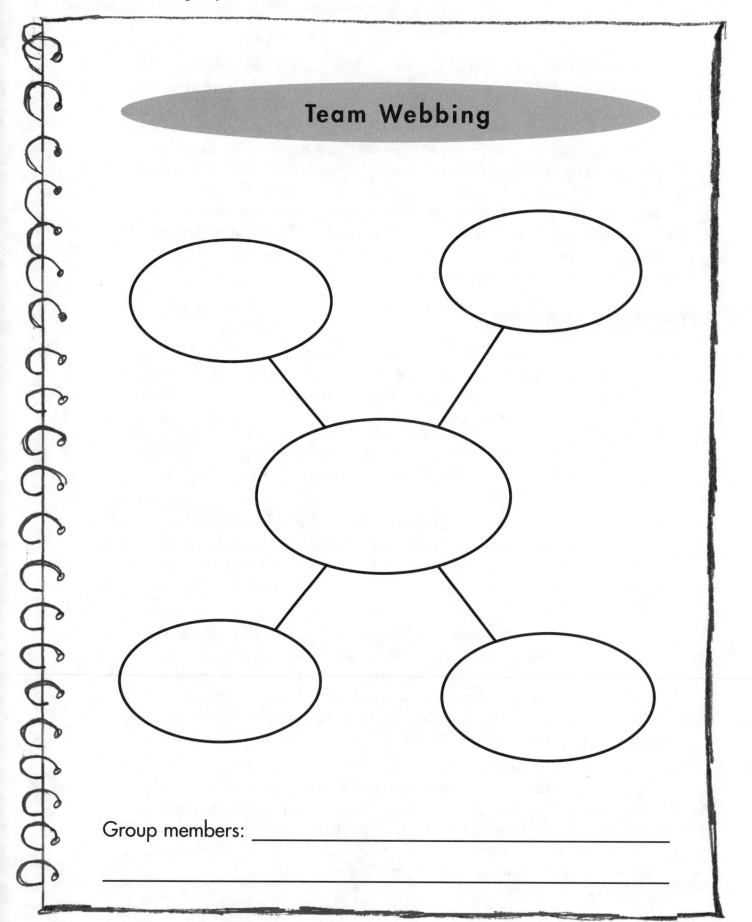

Team Webbing

Group members: _____

_____

Leonardo da Vinci, Renaissance Man

By Sean Price

Imagine that you are one of the world's greatest artists. On top of that, imagine that you are a pioneering inventor and a top-flight scientist, astronomer, architect, engineer, and costume designer. Sound pretty ambitious? Leonardo da Vinci (dah VIN-chee) managed to become all those things and a few more.

Leonardo, who lived from 1452 to 1519, is remembered as a genius largely because of his breathtaking paintings, such as the Mona Lisa and The Last Supper. However, his hungry mind made him an expert in many fields. Among other things, he drew plans for a flying machine and a parachute, created highly advanced maps and globes, invented musical instruments, and made the first serious study of flight. He also designed a self-closing toilet lid and a new, improved stink bomb.

Child of the Renaissance

Leonardo lived in a period known as the Renaissance (rehn-eh-SAHNS), which means "rebirth." It began about a.d. 1300 in Italy, and spread to northern and western Europe. It was a transition period from the Middle Ages (about a.d. 500 to 1500) to modern times.

During the Middle Ages, learn-

Easy Strategies and Mini-Lessons That Build Content Area Reading Skills Scholastic Professional Books, 1999

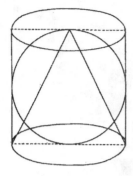

ing made little progress in Europe. Christian scholars concentrated on religion and the afterlife. Scientific discoveries were few and far between. As for art, even the best paintings looked stiff and unrealistic.

Then came the Renaissance, when Europe rediscovered the art and learning of ancient Greece and Rome. Much of that learning was rediscovered through trade with Muslim countries in the Middle East and North Africa. People there had preserved ancient works that earlier Europeans had discarded.

Those rediscovered works inspired fresh creativity in Europe. Northern Italy, where Leonardo lived, was the center of that creative drive. Leonardo was among the handful of brilliant men who led the way.

Small-Town Boy

Leonardo was born and raised near

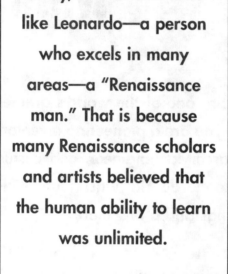

Today, we call someone like Leonardo—a person who excels in many areas—a "Renaissance man." That is because many Renaissance scholars and artists believed that the human ability to learn was unlimited.

the small town of Vinci (da Vinci means "of Vinci"), outside the city of Florence. He was the son of a wealthy man named Ser Piero, but little else is known about his childhood.

One surviving story hints that Leonardo's talent was recognized early on. The story has it that a peasant on Ser Piero's estate asked his landlord for a favor. He wanted Ser Piero to take a small wooden shield to Florence to have an image painted on it.

Instead of asking a professional artist to paint the shield, Ser Piero gave it to his teenage son. Leonardo took it and painted a monster from Greek mythology on it. Then the boy showed it to his father.

The painting was so realistic that it scared Ser Piero, who backed away in fear. "This work certainly serves its purpose," Leonardo told him. "It has produced the right reaction."

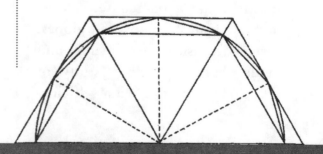

Easy Strategies and Mini-Lessons That Build Content Area Reading Skills Scholastic Professional Books, 1999

Talented Teenager

At about age 17, Leonardo became the apprentice (worker-in-training) to a famous artist in Florence. He finished his apprenticeship in about three years, but stayed on in Florence. Ten years later, the ruler of Milan (mee-LAHN) became the first of Leonardo's many patrons (wealthy supporters).

Milan was one of many city-states in northern Italy at the time. Political leaders—as well as wealthy merchants and bankers—made the Renaissance possible by supporting artists and scholars like Leonardo.

Renaissance Man

Today, we call someone like Leonardo—a person who excels in many areas—a "Renaissance man." That is because many Renaissance scholars and artists believed that the human ability to learn was unlimited. They tried to know all that there was to know.

Even during his lifetime, Leonardo was recognized as a well-rounded genius as well as a great artist. Wealthy people all over Europe begged him to paint their portraits.

Leonardo's best-known painting is the Mona Lisa. It was immediately recognized as a masterpiece for two major reasons. First, Leonardo made his subject look more like a flesh-and-blood person than any previous artist. Second, admirers were drawn to Mona Lisa's curious half-smile. From one angle, she appears to be content. From another, she seems to be smirking. From still other angles, she seems to have different expressions.

Practical Joker

Leonardo's personal life has become masked by countless legends. One thing that we do know about him is that he loved practical jokes. One time, he scared party guests by inflating the innards of a ram and letting them float into the next room.

Another thing we know is that he had a hard time finishing projects. Only about a dozen of his paintings are known to exist, and two are incomplete. Leonardo's habit of not finishing what he started was probably caused by the brilliance of his mind. Easily bored, he was always eager to move on to the next project.

He Wrote Backward

Although he made few paintings, Leonardo left behind hundreds of drawings. Many reflect his passion for science. He kept large notebooks filled with drawings and notes—his observations on such things as the behavior of

Easy Strategies and Mini-Lessons That Build Content Area Reading Skills Scholastic Professional Books, 1999

water and light.

Leonardo wrote in a backward script—for privacy, apparently: His notes could be read only by holding them up to a mirror. He planned to write books based on his notes and drawings.

Some of his scientific studies were tied to his work as an artist. For instance, he dissected (cut open and examined) human corpses so that he would be able to draw human forms accurately.

Leonardo's drawings and notes also show that he came close to making a major scientific discovery: understanding how the heart pumps blood through the body. But his inability to follow through kept him from being as great a scientist as he was an artist. Although he designed many advanced machines and made many ingenious observations, he seldom tested his ideas to see if they worked.

Leonardo never wrote the books that he planned either. His notebooks contained valuable information, but most of them remained unpublished until three centuries after his death. Some experts believe that up to 75 percent of his works have been lost forever.

Leonardo's Legacy

Despite that, Leonardo's influence is with us still. His small group of paintings made a huge impact. Today, we take for granted the lifelike art that he helped pioneer. In science, Leonardo's techniques for drawing human anatomy (body structure) revolutionized medical studies and are still used today.

Also, thanks to Leonardo and other Renaissance leaders, our store of knowledge has grown tremendously. In fact, it has grown so much that it is difficult for anyone today to master many fields of knowledge and become a Renaissance man or woman.

Although Leonardo planned more than he could finish, it is impossible to ignore the genius of what he planned. As Leonardo's first biographer wrote 500 years ago, "His name and fame will never be extinguished."

"Leonardo da Vinci, Renaissance Man" originally appeared in Junior Scholastic, February 7, 1997.

Easy Strategies and Mini-Lessons That Build Content Area Reading Skills Scholastic Professional Books, 1999